NORTHERN FIELDS

Other Books by Chuck Miller

NORTHERN FIELDS

NEW & SELECTED POEMS BY CHUCK MILLER

COFFEE HOUSE PRESS :: MINNEAPOLIS :: 1994

The author thanks the editors of the following magazines and publishing houses where many of these works first appeared: *Caprice* and *World Letter* magazines, Friends Press, Seamark Press. "for Barbara," "for Schnu," "Free Clinic," "lighted windows (for Judy)," and "when you live in your car" were published by The Spirit That Moves Us Press in *How In The Morning: Poems 1962-1988,* by Chuck Miller, in 1988.

The publishers would like to thank the following funders for assistance which helped make this book possible: The Bush Foundation; The Dayton Hudson Foundation on behalf of Dayton's and Target Stores; The National Endowment for the Arts, a Federal Agency; The General Mills Foundation; The Jerome Foundation; The Lannan Foundation; The Andrew W. Mellon Foundation; The Beverly J. and John A. Rollwagen Fund of the Minneapolis Foundation; Star Tribune/Cowles Media Company; and The McKnight Foundation. This activity is made possible in part by a grant provided by the Minnesota State Arts Board, through an appropriation by the Minnesota State Legislature. Major new marketing initiatives have been made possible by the Lila Wallace–Reader's Digest Literary Publishers Marketing Development Program, funded through a grant to the Council of Literary Magazines and Presses.

Coffee House Press books are available to the trade through our primary distributor, Consortium Book Sales & Distribution, 1045 Westgate Drive, Saint Paul, MN 55114. Our books are also available through all major library distributors and jobbers, and through most small press distributors, including Bookpeople, Inland, and Small Press Distribution. For personal orders, catalogs or other information, write to:

Coffee House Press
27 North Fourth Street, Suite 400, Minneapolis, MN 55401

Library of Congress CIP Data
Miller, Chuck, 1939–
    Northern fields: poems / by Chuck Miller.
       p.   cm.
    ISBN 1-56689-014-4 (pbk.)
    I. Title.
PS3563.137653N67   1993
813'.54—dc20   93–26007,CIP

10   9   8   7   6   5   4   3   2   1

Table of Contents

For Jim and Heidi

late September

you wake slowly without abruptness
as though there were no line between sleep and consciousness
and see the leaves variegate the woodland floor
in some diagonal drift,
gray skies with the smell of wetness in the air
the flurries of wind sound
as though your relatives were arguing again
in the trees,
but in truth their arguments have ceased
for some stopped with earth
and you remember that yesterday
suddenly in a moment of consciousness
you could not speak on the surface of things
there was only a feeling
a long grasp of memory
and now that too has passed

the birds make insistencies with their cries
and you wait for the water to boil
to wash the dishes
think of the trees that fell last night on the farm
and your dog asleep in her place
practicing perhaps
for the long sleep not long to come

start up the music again

dawn coming
the roosters call in the distance
like tiny spumes sent up
an intimate awakening
realizing slowly that it's been some time
since they crowed in my morning
hearing them, puts you back
as though the earth were alive

the currents come
with their turnings and nudges
you think, i am in my own bed
in my own house
in this particular small life
and however strange this may be
it might also be common, average
yet with some amplitude
enough so that
there is some room to breathe
some time to live
no mortgage on this shack . . .

but there is a hunger
for those other times
when if we were more desperate for everything
we were also more alive
in some other way,
you seek out this sense
without knowing how
exactly you are going about it

but what is it
. . . the memory of our lost youth . . .
or something generational
that now seems almost past for us
or that once we struck out against them
and made a life, at least for a while
so completely different
than their own

or that most real thing
which we will find again
or not live

"if you can't make a joke . . ."

"if you can't make a joke . . .
if you can't have a laugh
with some people
sometime . . ."
he was laughing with us, a table away
with the joke he heard us make
spoke slowly and with great awkwardness
"then . . . then . . ."
a Norse troll, or déclassé Finnish woodworker
in image, something of the troglodyte
and archaic . . . as though he were his own grandfather
from the old country . . . maybe north of Trondheim
but now even more out of place
in the hokey modern world
i came over to sit with him
"some people
some people they don't care about people
they're troublemakers
and they don't change
they'll be that way . . . and the best thing is
just to keep to yourself . . .
"the best thing" . . . , as though letting me in on a secret
"keep to yourself"
misshapen, he looked like a human totem
from the backwoods of the Arctic Circle,
a real *skraelling* in some classist, Marxist sense
now in the new land
forgotten whatever origin where he might have been at home
dusted lightly with age
"most people are nice . . .
but they'll always be some" his voice rose in a kind of emphasis

"some from where you are,"
his mouth working now, to articulate these more extensive
    remarks
"and some from where you're going
I know, I've been around . . . they'll be there"
shaking his head up and down at the truth of it
and looking grimly off into the distance

i thought of the trouble this guy had seen
and of Munch and his half-formed people in that stained light
the horizontally lined skies and the ultimate north at their backs

some gave him a wide berth
but he joked with one of the waitresses
about knowing the other one for three weeks now
she treated him with a patient studied kindness
as he struggled to speak each syllable
each one labored but still a little indistinct
hard to catch
it seems as though i was his student
is this true, i wondered

"these people . . .
they fouled up my work
and I can't say more than that . . . I'll just
politely . . . you see . . . I can't say more than that
next month it'll come up in court"
it seemed he had been a kind of janitor or maintenance worker
and these people had thrown a monkey wrench in his tasks

"they never learn . . . these people"
and you thought of the ones high and low
for whom that would be true

"you'll always find them . . . anywhere"
saying this with great earnestness . . . trying to inform us
of this cogent lesson
he knew by heart . . . his own
. . . listening intently
realizing how strange but fortunate it seemed
that people came and taught me their lessons
had i really heard though, what he was trying to impart?
this story . . . almost like some truncated myth
which seemed my own already
even as he told it
but something in me wants to argue with him
that something has to be done . . . challenge taken up
but you had seen how useless all that was
except maybe inside yourself

this guy . . . actually he seemed steady . . . level
and as the days passed . . . and you saw him in the same Café
and in the street . . . making his way, talking with people
enjoying his lunch . . .
you realized he had made a life for himself
his freakishness dropped away
here was a human looking out on the world
an ancestor sent from the land of silence and darkness
to travel along
make the strange migrations
with the rest of us
troublemakers
and to-oneself keepers

Skraelling: word the Norse used for Eskimos or Indians or whoever it was they
met and deemed less elite than themselves; literally "babbler," or "screamer."

14

"some days"

some days
the sunlight has a clarity
it's as though our flesh were balanced by it
our memory struck back through the years

we seem erect mammals walking on the earth,
if puffs of dust rise from our steps
it's this which keeps our cadence
it's this which makes our pattycakes

if my old dog also seems friskier
on these days
if, in her old, old age
she takes spark again
and starts to run, actually run
over the ploughed fields
as though everything could be brought back again unmangled
it's for this we keep thinking
it's for this we ourselves would come running over the fields

putting up snow fence

we are ghosts on the plains of November
from some far eye's distance
or perhaps as if we were in that distance
against a dun ridge, climbing, near the crest
almost able to touch the clouds
yet in another longer perspective, static
moving but as if unmoved—
along our sloping field we trudge like small stickmen
on this immense plain
putting up snow fence
to fence the snow in   or out
against the drifts
not yet born

pounding with the stake-driver
again and again
Sisyphus our jokey friend
looking back at the long row
like the lineman
down the singleness of his trail,
to see if it's buckled or held

twisting the wire ties
between the stakes and the fence
like fate twisting us
along some corkscrewy journey
the galvanized ones making us curse
and cry out

i look at the sun opening to us
from the sullen sky
some clear passage through
and remember some twenty years past
when i saw god, face to face
yet there was no face—
and then mulling the silences
between our cold breathing
and mist formulations
"but this was the illegal god"

the opening passes
and the sky closes on its grey promises
and again i am downwind
as though i had never left
that prison farm of years ago
but rather it grew
spreading instead, like mold
on a piece of bread
to engulf town after community
until encompassing some other
archipelago

* * *

rolling the fence-rolls along
or kicking them to their places
like some game you played as a boy
to keep the momentum going
—kicking a tin can down a road

but now forty years later
still along the same *strada*
following after
the road more barren, the can more absurd

to open once more,
leave behind
the stickman
sentenced so long ago
to what labors we barely fathom

strada: road (Italian)

"riding the bus in the evening again"

riding the bus in the evening again
home to my place in the woods
you get a closer look at what's left of them
after the workday extracts its measure
some manage to talk distractedly
most stare silently with that numbed look
only two small brown foreigners
manage to keep a dream alive
talking with shy animation to each other
perhaps they are still escalating up the dream ladder
and haven't yet met it face to face
on some grisly morning,
one stares at the writing
on the bottle of his psychotropic drugs
as though what it says there will explain it all
the driver take us
through the shoals of traffic
the afternoon sun
on the sundial of our faces
telling the lateness of the hour
remembering an old friend in Chicago
who died of an overdose
trying to explain the people there
they were, he said, like "damaged goods"

and these, their faces vacant
bodies splayed out and tumorous with fat,
slumped with fatigue
they hoist themselves up to the door
sizing up where they will alight
as the bus brakes and slows to stop,

and then as it pulls away
i see them look off, perhaps up the road
or back down it
before they cross
toward the supermarket
where they will buy with hundreds of others
their evening repast of artificial foods and chemicals,
to sit in front of their televisions
as their lives pale into a deeper shade of gray
having made it, as it is said
through another day

for Mickey

in the corncrib you remember
the strange light and dark alternations
some older structure
from a more primitive memory sense
house of dreams where the sky comes through
yet intricately shadowed and enclosed
hear the wind again crying
coming in under the door
the old north wind they called it
moaning in that long drawn-out . . .
sifting as it sang
maybe some being nosing in
not like the wild cat who lived in their barn
as you might have thought as a child
or some dog coming wet and hungry from the timber
nuzzling up from the open bottom half of the barn door
but almost conscious it might have seemed
like some old gray spirit searching lost . . .
saying "who you, muteboy?"
but so everlasting through the corn stubble
coming from the far fields
in unending passage
that seemed so mysterious and telling
yet what foretold?

and seeing the corn between the slats in those earlier years
some shocks husked in with them
how did the animals eat it . . . you wondered . . . like food
    made of stone
do we too harden in such a way?
"what if it snowed?" you asked your friend

"snow or rain, the air still dried it out"
and in the barn you remembered plunging into the oat bin
and sinking down nut-deep
as in some still dry sea caught
so pungent, deep, and quietly evocative
some hermetic sense as though here you found the essence
but of what you could not have said . . .
perhaps the treasures they hide away
and lose from lack of use . . .

"once I came in here and the squirrel first ran that way
and then back
he must have had it all planned
because then he jumped in that metal chute you see
and I could hear him sliding down it all the way over to there
where he popped out
but then another time at night
I shined the flashlight straight up there at the top
to where the gabled window is
and I saw two huge greenish-yellow eyes staring down at me
an owl, he didn't move, but just looked at me
I'd hate to be a little animal, and see those eyes
those green lantern eyes just looked straight into me
and didn't move"
he showed me how they had put old license plates
under the eaves to keep the boards from rotting out
starting with 1920, 1921 . . .
it reminded me of how they used to insulate their houses
old newspapers between the studs
everything utilized in their sparse economies
but maybe you think putting distance, time
and the world in the fabric of their houses
in some patterned sense—like papering their walls with history

the passage of the years recorded?
no, laughing to yourself, reminding . . .
just practicality that's all

cutting down small trees that have grown up
within inches of the crib
and you almost forget you are destroying live things
then bending down to touch a stump
as though to say what? what excuse can you give
or do you need one? never quite sure
of what you are really doing

working till late afternoon, we go back to the house
the sidewalk around the porch, uneven slabs articulating
    crookedly
some tree root pushing up from under, that too
reminding me of the old place
and inside the .22 lying across the freezer
the house and its inner arrangement
separated, removed, almost formal
just as the ones you remember

sitting in the dining room drinking a cold glass of water
you lean back in the rocking chair
and through the window
you see the sun on the white clapboard
a pure, austere, and brilliant white
and in this bare intensity
imagine what can be transformed
yet always with such difficulty, almost grudgingly . . .
yourself . . . relationships . . . things are as they are

and remember that old one
"you can't make a silk purse out of a sow's ear"
they used to say
with that harsh glint in their voices

perhaps you could have lived this life
in whose sphere you began
whose symbols strike you so powerfully
the old barn, how beautiful it was
the roof caving back to some nonlinear
more organic form . . .
the straightforward work
taking the wood to the brushpile
on the way home in the pickup
you both are tired and peaceful
and feel a sense of all the senses intermingled
and how perhaps we had beat them in some way
those who castigated us for what we were
or should have been
and who compelled us to suffer
on pain of whatever they could lash us with

. . . escaped into the air
live in the house of slats
where the sky comes in

"in the typewriter shop"

in the typewriter shop
the owner has been poring over maps
before my interruption

tells me how he plans trips
although he may not
probably won't take them
because it's
not so satisfying traveling alone now

shows me the different ways
he's been to Thunder Bay
and Isle Royale
routes across the Upper Peninsula
but mostly, of late, he goes to Las Vegas
hard for me to grasp, this last

a gray-haired modest man
moves about his shop
like some more modern
shoemaker
that solid, workmanlike presence
but more intricate his tasks
and lonelinesses perhaps

gives me good advice
tells me why he doesn't carry typing paper now
the price jumped double
for no discernible reason he knew

does he look
for a shy older woman at the slots?

offers me a deal on my three old broken 'writers
for a good, clean, used one
that maybe i might go for

a human animal in a useful cage
sage, aging
his tidy virtues clear
and almost singing a small inaudible song

thus we walk about in the gray day
probing in our strange revolutions to survive
seeing occasionally
a leftover sense of human presence undisintegrated

"wondered why the building was so small"

wondered why the building was so small
for an electric company?
and the multitude of employee cars ranged round. . . ?
filling out the forms, i was still under the delusion
it had something to do with electricity, my first
but abandoned love,
and maybe i could learn something—
the employment manager said "telemarketing . . ."
and i pretended to keep smiling
"and how do you think you'd like
this kind of work. . . ?" in her mechanical voice
she could probably spot me a mile off
but the place must have a high turnover . . .
in a jagged instant that cut deep inside me
i decided that if they hired me
i'd go till the evaluation cutoff point
as they paid an hourly wage
rather than commission
collecting a kind of evidence
and trying to get it down—
she took me to the workroom and opened the door
i tried to muffle the immediate revulsion i felt
a sanitized version of bedlam or the snakepit
people heaped up on top of one another
in a windowless room
each wearing earphones
and looking into their "terminal," jabbering on and on
it wasn't hard it seemed
to find a great many desperate enough to prostitute themselves

whether they knew it or not
for five dollars an hour
and yet, you surmised, it probably represented
some kind of "real" opportunity for them
not electricity or its elaborations made here
but capitalism, jammed in claustrophobic tangle
there was a girl at a little blackboard
in each area, marking up tallies
"good job, so-and-so," i heard her say
and you got the Pavlovian drift
petty squad leaders shooting coercive propaganda at you
"there's quota in your turf . . ."
and similar inanities
"and what do you think . . ."
still considering that I might hack it
for a few weeks pay
and what you could make of it in some subversive way
i made ambiguous reply
"you'll be hearing from us . . ." she said
and i didn't doubt it . . . in one sense or another
finding my car in the lot
hoped that beater would start
so i could get the hell out fast
as usual looking for work was a bad joke
but at least you didn't take it so seriously
as when you were young
but there might come a day
and not so very distant
when you'd have to take it very seriously indeed
they ought to pay me, it comes to you
in some absurd aside to yourself

to speak to first graders
and let them in on what this life has planned for them
i begin to elaborate my "primary lectures"
as the beater hits a dip too fast
and think it may have knocked up the oilpan or radiator
but it keeps going

dead dog (for goo)

walking by the edge of the woods across the crest of the hill
the wind whips down from the east
the snow blows up in tiny hard bits
i realize again that i should have
brought my dog back
dug into the frozen earth
and put her here in the ground
under the woods where she'd sometimes nose about

one day she keeled over
or would walk crookedly in contradictory directions
something in her eyes
as though she knew it already, saw it
or perhaps it was i saw it in her eyes . . .
then she got a little better, looked at me
as though clearly wondering, and ate a little again

she seemed no longer afraid at the veterinarian's
and almost lucid at the end
as though in some last stage, mild and aware
responding to my touch
they opened her up
and found cancer all through the liver
so accordingly
put her to death before she woke

i had gotten her from the dental labs
before they put them to sleep
she was a yappy skittery thing as a pup
a wiry paranoid rat terrier
going a thousand miles an hour in every direction

jumping up on everyone by way of greeting
with the little black feet of excitement
as though tap-dancing claw-dancing
ticker-ticker on the old linoleum

she'd frequently run off
and wander back looking entirely innocent
as though "who me?"
we had plenty of conflicts
her balking act when we'd go for a walk
when she'd sense too sharp an angle to our circumnavigation
that meant back too soon . . .
and her hunger strikes where finally
one or the other of us would give in,
perhaps she was more right than i knew

almost entirely black
except for a few white spots
on summer nights when i'd be looking for her
i'd look for a piece of blackness
a little darker than the night
but in the end . . . her muzzle had gone all gray

generally she'd shy away from fights
but when forced into them was a formidable opponent
i could remember my girlfriend prying open her jaws
with her hands
to get her to let go
of her dog's throat

strange, yet it makes sense
that they have been our companions since neolithic
our first friend
and domestic animal in this estranged world

in her old age she seemed to wise up
no longer fought, and other dogs seemed to sense it
seemed much more affectionate
in her look sometimes you'd see what it was about
a sense of calm sadness, resignation perhaps
but as though it was no longer of any significance
. . . then she'd get up and examine everything again
as though no less curious than in her youth

by the end i felt we knew each other
better than most humans . . .
the only other being
who was clearly "mine" in some way

it dawns on us too slowly perhaps
that life is a series of disappearances
. . . from a sense of seeing too late
i feel the mystery and grief
of this comrade gone into the unknown

the wind

some days the wind comes
stronger than ourselves
and our intentions,
yet we identify with this invisible passage
the creaking of the limbs, the crooked straining of the branches
—a corner of our discontent is sent spinning
and then something in us rises up ravening

and this rising and falling, almost oceanic, circadian
so like our own sense of things,
and as it dies away
muttering to the dead sticks
haunting and grieving over the fallow fields
guttering at last down the corroded throat of loss

but then slowly, leaf by leaf
it up picks anew
back again from the dead
agitating now an old soliloquy without words
coming then full force
no less than a sounding of our lyric aspiration
and even more of our searching desire
. . . lest we imagine that we too
could sing at such a pitch . . .

listening in to it
we think there must be still
autumn storms to rake over our sleep
and March blows to wake us forever

the old north wind
blows down on us
we see its burning visage still
in our ash heap hearts

for those who pray for the souls of broken dolls

only the Japanese, the narrator said
who animate objects and things
give them credit for some life of their own . . .
armless
footless
with only one eye staring glassily up at us
broken necks
tiny soiled dolls' skirts
the stuffing coming out
you imagine them found in some dump
rolled over
ripped apart
but now retrieved, collected
for these last rites . . .
these strange images of ourselves
but no, beings in their own right
just as we in our way . . .
with souls no less
of wood perhaps, totem souls . . .
or given to them
by those that once cherished . . .

now they heap them up on a pyre and light it
all merging in one flaming rubble heap
and these few Japanese pray then
you see them drop their heads slightly
as in sadness or reverence
pray for the souls of broken dolls

northern fields (for Carol)

you have to smile
coming on them again
more bare   perhaps by now somewhat poisoned
but your own   in some intangible sense
the trees perhaps a little taller
to get more of that tilted sun?
you'd been roaming   the southern spaces
Kansas and the Kaw   down through Oklahoma
watching tugs bringing up the barges
in the blinking blue-green night
Tennessee into the moonlit meadows of Kentucky
now back to the north
you watch the wind moving whole skies across the plains
the gloomy woods flash by
little towns more austere
and likewise the fields
that thrill of recognition—
somewhat barren and remote
autumn coming earlier and fiercer
the people with that stoic in their look,
some of them sense
the hidden life
the rain comes beating gray and transparent on the off-green
    crops
the wood edging the horizon
distant treeline
or last window,
frail brushwork on all we will ever know of infinity
the bitter sour wetness on the wind blowing in on us
making us laugh
and with a taste of irony

at this slightly preposterous identification
as though we were the ones finally
who had learned to love these harder places
that these fields
this sparseness
should be ours

on getting my poems back from the typist

seeing them again, now in their final form
so clearly arranged, untangled and sorted out
it comes to you; nearly meaningless
queer that you should feel so little anguish
but rather just that it's clearly so

and how strange and futile, almost laughable
that all the work of it, the struggle hashed out
should come to so little . . .

when our bones crumble with the earth
and we are one with it, the dirt
in the long run perhaps only
that we tried to express something . . .
and for the women you were with
not how it ended or who fucked it up
but somewhere along the line
did you put something into it . . .

for literature
that some of what was said
meant something to a few of us
if only fleetingly
no matter which end of it you were on

yet could seeing this meagerness of meaning now
bring you closer to what you were trying for
by clearing away certain blocks and vanities?
a supposition, that
in your ignorance . . .
and like so many other suppositions,
of dubious validity and likely to go astray

how apparent all this seems
and like some weird new clear perception
might lead us
leads us, through the mirror maze
now redoubling itself
by some chain of antimeaning

"swimming in the last of September"

swimming in the last of September
you come alive again
a slender warm current playing against the cold of the medium
at first you think you can't stand it
but little by little . . .
you force yourself to tolerate it
and your body comes round . . .
by the time you get out
the water seems relatively mild . . . or almost
on the bank forget your clothes
and stand struck . . .
naked as an animal and are you not?
memories come back
from the yellow tops of trees
as though from some high transom of the air
the sun and leaves radiant on you
a primitive human again
or were you ever anything else?
almost as though from the objectified world you had broken
    out
as through a crust of ice
and regrounded your subjectivity,
in a few minutes standing before the tumble of rocks
the hidden sources again seem revealed
and it is dawning on you
as it always should have been dawning
the crucial mystery . . .
but you can see
that snatching back what you can a little a day
is not enough . . .
but for a time you're not breathing the chemical air

your feet are soft in the dirt again
or touch firm on the rock
as the dog bounds up the hill in crisscross
the prairie spreads out before you
you could almost reach out
gesture to it, pull it in

and then going from little grove to little grove
along a dry streambed
you forget everything from moment to moment
as in an old acid memory
where being revealed itself to you
each tree or bush or dry ditch was speaking to us
in some language of light and existence
of the fundamental innocence and wisdom of things

semantic drift

the basic ones don't seem to change much
during this microinterval
in terms of some radical shift or evolution,
rather they change by wearing out
take "love"
you still use it
but it doesn't quite muster
or the curses
no matter how often you used them
pounding with their tiny hammers
against the sea's roar
they lost their edge
and you never quite expressed
your final bitterness
now they seem almost innocuous
yet a few good "fucks"
can still get you in a lot of trouble
seeming still obscene to some
even rarely sometimes to yourself
"friendship" too seems blown over
with drifted earth
or moved on
like a tumbleweed
the other ones
like little pebbles
we trade back and forth
in an absurd pantomime
of what life should be
as for the complex, extraordinary, or beautiful ones
there is so little opportunity to use them
in a context in which they would live up to their meanings

that we let them loose like wild horses
to go back where they came from
and for the rest
what can we say
something gives way
slowly, inevitably
as if they were built over an old mine
and were gradually falling in,
for daily life
the ones that are left
are like old money the mint is about to repossess
the mint here being God, or the earth
but, for the time being,
they are still our "ill-legal tender"
and will have to do
for whatever poor meanings
we can summon up

near Old Fort Pike on the Des Moines River

the way the light
on the low, flat sandbanks
now come out of the diminished river, strikes this morning
some birds further downstream, pigeon-colored
for the most part——only one white one
barely moving in silent colloquy, gathered round
on a bank—almost as if in church

upstream the bluffs rise dark
on the Missouri side,
the beige weeds just upriver
and on the further bars
reedlike, wheatlike
"a crop grown on a temporary island"

just this
no great beauty
but some sense
of moving toward what exists
free for the perceiving
this fresh-light morning, on the running brown water
some inner core of vision cut out of us
or grown back?

the dog senses something
and lies down in the shallow streambed
pleased to be performing his ablutions
no church for him

"they came furtively"

they came furtively
like a little band of outsiders on the run
maybe four of them beyond the fence bordering the woods
stood at different intervals
between the small ditch and its few little trees
and the windrow—white-tails probably
though i didn't notice that
but rather how they paused and looked at me
in the lavender twilight
with such inquisitiveness—
in a dream-time almost dark so that sight was failing
we stood and gazed as long as we could
so tranced and quiet they had a kind of spell
as though we were holding on
to some unspoken thing between us
i felt if i moved it would be lost
was i "one of those" they might have thought
who troubled them so greatly—
but instead they seemed curious, communicative—
such gentleness
as though they might have considered
as in the old Indian belief
offering themselves so that i could eat
yet in a sudden fluid movement they were gone
moving across the darkness of the field

later, thinking about it
it almost seemed a kind of visitation
like a few dreams i could remember
where someone had come back from years before
smiled at you enigmatically with a kind of tenderness

laughed once
put their arms around you briefly
then disappeared

the end of the negotiable beggar bond banquet

a fight at the welfare office again
"just like old times . . ." i laughingly tell my friends
hadn't been there in several years
big brother and big sister a little snoopier than before
and now they want to force you to see a film on how to get
    food stamps
as if i didn't know already
an insult to our intelligence
and besides it's against my religion
the cretinous clerks at the front desk the first line of defense
then the smoother bourgeois gals come out of their offices
as i wander through trying to find someone who will listen to me
"WHAT are you DOING back here . . . would you PLEASE go
    out front . . ."
then one of the few male workers acting the rooster whose hens
    have been riled
as if he were offended not only by your presence
but by your very existence . . .
you're like a cow who broke out of the chutes at the
    slaughterhouse
and now you're wandering around mooing and kicking up
    your heels

between fits of shouting back and forth
i try to explain to them that i've got to be at work
and can't waste time on their film
"no, you've got to see this film
and it'll take about two hours . . ."
lording it over you in their smarty-pants way
"otherwise you won't get your stamps . . ."
the power of food or no food

in their cold indifferent mugs . . .
all the same old crew again
collecting their money for degrading and humiliating us
looking down their nose
as though you were some sort of psychopath,
acting as the agents for the big stooges and criminals in
    Washington
who are spending your taxes killing and intimidating people all
    over the earth
now with some new plan again, a new adjustment
meaning they think they've figured out a better way to put the
    screws to us . . .
you wonder what it would be like
to really go berserk some day
trash their office screaming and bellowing
give them something to gossip about with their neighbors
"he was so weird looking and dressed funny . . .
i knew there was something crazy about him . . ."
they'd call the pigs and beat you—
pitted scum against scum
the bitterness drives deeper in you
remember all over again why you are an anarchist

go through the arguments once more
on violence versus nonviolence
like rifling quickly through a pack of cards
maybe nonviolence winning by a nose
but too close for comfort
you think it will probably depend more on accidental
    circumstance
which way it would fall

maybe when you see some cop using his stick upside the head
  of some gentle soul
the blood rippling out
the brutal snarl on the pig's face embedded there forever in
  your retina

finally leave, slamming the front door
like some steer that has been cattle-prodded
a little punchy and disoriented
remembering how you told yourself
you'd make a new effort not to let your anger
get the better of you

but in some other way it drifts up to you
that although this might be a leaner month
there's still something alive inside
a blind instinct that refuses to give in
a bitterness
that will try to go the distance

flood

although we curse the dreary weather
and feel some apprehension
as the drenching cloudbursts come down
the sky so thick with gray rain
that visibility drops sharply off

nonetheless when we see the ditches running full of brown
    water
lip of lace mad foam in its leaping chaos run
and sense underneath that power coursing
smelling the fresh earth smell
something in us thrills

glad to see the deep strength of nature assert itself
as though briefly enabling us
to imagine overflowing our own banks
breaking our inner bonds
and flowing out over the fields
and through the forests
unfettered by the constraints
of our absurd and malign civilization

and under the bridges and through the narrows
we see that turgid raging
we must look into its depth
as though seeing there
what has long been denied us

under the trees
and through the speckled leaves in the flooded woodland
the sunset fringes darker shadows
the silvering stream now broadening out
as though opening a way

and the next day
not sure if the river has crested
we look down from the bridge into its massive movement
as though the earth itself moved under us
a cold fluid lava two-thirds akin to us
and the voice of this great water beast
pitched low yet ominous in its softswift murmur
half frightened and half hopeful
wishing perhaps
that it would sweep away
this detritus life
and make us whole and free again

but we think of broken-off tree trunks
the ruin in their branches desolate in prehistoric splendor
planks from splintered houses
river-bottom farms a sea of watery waste

all floating in the river's silent oblivion abandon
or bodies drifting face down
in some flood of years ago
our ancestors bleak-faced in flat-bottomed boats
now doubly gray into gray infinity
poling their way through some unknown lost slough
bedraggled family huddled in the bottom by the gunwales

in the silent cycles of generations
along the rivers of where we might be heading
still mysterious and unknown

dusk in the woods

the woods in one half of my binocular vision
the radio flowering in the other now almost nonmovable ear
reflecting the fire-storm world
epidemics of murder to the south
great chords of propaganda struck from "the tower of truth"
coming to the end of our branch perhaps
on the bush of evolution
the last species of hominids extant,
our opposable thumb
our expanded cranial capacity
not enough to shove in the breach,
unable to conceive of a solution
other than the small human gestures we might make
and these not enough
perhaps if our sense of smell—so closely linked
to our instinctual feelings—
had not atrophied—
does this make any sense?

anarchist perhaps just a word
that sloughs off like a skin,
as governments convulse and disintegrate
many will become anarchists of a sort before the end
without knowing enough of what it tried to mean

where now is your anger at all this
your protective rage
against being cheated
ripped off
oppressed?
somehow you too have contributed to this immeasurable
    failure,

understanding too vulnerable in its newbornness
ignorance too frail
in this shifting mixture

listening to the voices
as they flare on in the voice-catcher
some of them—like lights
turning up in the dusk
such lucidity and compassion
—yet probably
not enough

dark coming in the little woods
the diurnal animals return to their hideaways
the dusky nestling—in among the leaves
so softly, so gently
what more poignant than this
ultimately they must depend on us
for their survival
pity them for that

the cold sense of autumn evening
sight dimming
this hopelessness wrenching me
the dark tide coming in

dislocado

a whole new town of them, *dislocados* from the war
Mozambicans it turns out from the radio report
these strange Africans speaking Portuguese
more and more of them made homeless by Renamo attacks
relatives killed and your own country funding the terrorists
and then the others for their various reasons
you can hear the dogs kicking up a ruckus, the sounds
of someone making breakfast, it's as though
they're camping right beside you . . .
spilling over and mingling with all the other displaced peoples
those living on the road
or at the edge of garbage dumps
or cities—coming to be the same
lucky to find a place maybe
in the shanty towns and *favelas*
how they pass through your mind
with their silences
their few words
is it they can't convey their experiences
or if they would
not to be understood—useless?
or worth only a few muttered words
spoken to the wind
but it rings inside you
as if it were some Esperanto word
immediately comprehensible when you hear it
too many times "dis-lodged" physically and otherwise
in too many estranged ways

different kinds you feel mingling into one essential sense
traveling wordlessly under the trees
moving off along the roads
disappearing in cities
into the brush

Renamo: byname of Mozambican National Resistance
favela: slum (Portuguese)

for Barbara

standing up eating a pan of oatmeal and rice
balanced on the top of the woodstove
—like an animal eating his food on the ground—
i am getting lost in the woods
bit by bit something gives way,
like a fox hiding in the grass
making his way along the edge of the field near the timber
the weird grimace almost becoming like a smile on his face

one day we'll come out on the plain
that leads to the river
we'll walk in the sun
at first we won't be sure if it's the river
then we'll know the broad beautiful expanse
we'll discover the lay of the land at last
in a shimmering silence
and long wood-knock-over-water echo
we'll become Cro-Magnon or Middle-Mississippian
turning up in some other life
and then looking back see the equally strange contours
of an old existence

and i don't really know
but just a queer sense
that leads a little further
and then edging along
although it might almost be gone,
the will-o'-the-wisp
that leads you out of or into the forest
listening to the voices . . . as they trail off
—in the margins
you talk to those who are no longer here

"saw 'er at a temple . . ."

saw 'er at a temple on the outskirts of Hangzhou
a stylish Chinese gal maybe 35 or 40
a bit hardened in her lipsticked face
plenty of moxie though it might have seemed
with her high heels, knowing sophisticated air
and loose Western skirt
that did not hide nonetheless
the allure of her lithe and shapely ass,
in front of the temple where she stood
some joss sticks burned in a metal smoker
from inside a giant golden Buddha looked calmly out
through the haze of Maya and delusion,
click-clacking over to the outer wall
a distance away from the large entrance,
she stopped almost facing it but turned away from the crowds
and looked back half furtively, half brazen
as if she might have been considering taking a pee
or having it off standing against the wall à la Swensk
instead she hiked up her skirt in front
and with a choice gesture reached up into her golden triangle
and started fishing out yuan notes of different colors
as though from her sacred cave drawing forth manna
i had seen this a few times before
and knew they sometimes strapped their money belts just
    there
she passed them on a handful at a time
to her husband or boyfriend, some smooth-faced con artist
gangster or political opportunist
with a glance of deep collusion
a queer intent concentration on her face
as she brought up more handfuls from her cache

like a kind of sexual magician
uprooting them from where they grew,
a hooker, i wondered
no, some more cunning and devious hustle, you surmised
as befits this corrupt country,
finished, she smoothed her dress
and shook herself like a cat
lit a package of incense sticks
then followed her man over to where the Buddha smiled
    benignly out
his lidded eyes and thumb-to-fingers meditation posture
her guy threw some handfuls of money in the collection box
maybe the monks who were the temple attendants
would eat a little better tonight
but what the Buddha persona would be thinking of it all
or if at all . . .
but here seemed confluence of sex, superstition
money and religion, and maybe politics or crime
all so smoothly concatenating together
hardly a ripple
yet still something grotesque and almost hallucinatory
as the symbolism of the gesture becomes emblazoned rite
and the images fuse into a kind of flickering glyph

they took their turns along with the others
kneeling and bowing down till their foreheads touched
the worn stone floor
just as their ancestors might have done it generations before
and as she knelt and bent over in supplication
paying her homage to old Guatama
her lovely magic ass bloomed up at me
a kind of heart-shaped flower
who knows, praying for their souls
or for some scam or ripoff to come through

Albina

mocking hooligan laughing down your hooligan days
but so much tenderness, yet rife with contradictions
free of the undertow of death fears
since as a child you had already encountered—
accepted—swept your face with its wing
leaving you a kind of precocious indifference
and so you spend yourself with some disregard
fatalist, you say "we meet only to part"
jesting much and crying rarely
you open yourself to me and i see the depth of your sorrow
climbing the small Chinese mountains you clamber up
    recklessly
leaving me behind stumbling and breathing hard
dancing then on the peaks alone

your mother, the fierce old polska *pani*
had said how could she whelp such a hooligan girl
joking or serious even you could not tell
i give you a make-believe name from your language
"cogda," meaning "when"
"too harsh sounding" you reply
but give me back *"potchemutchka,"* "why-pesterer"
with love, you say
you never know why
only that it is—
teacher, "Miss Pedagogue" that i tease you with
formalist, nonetheless a real *"kobieta literatury"*
ihr Russisch nichtunguter Name—to begin or does it end
in the same incomplete gesture

between the irrevocable and different *"cogdas"*
a blood seismograph stutters our intermittent tremors and
    sorrows

i stand you back out of time
and see you always in that "moment cut out of sequence"
laughing, gesturing, mocking
a storyteller's story we are weaving
speaking between us a crisscross of broken languages

finally your destitute sadness
some lonely Siberian river flooding in spring
without a name
then we become like the rocks
our speech changed into "only a glance in the sky"

pani: lady (Polish)
kobieta literatury: woman of literature (Polish)
ihr Russisch nichtunguter Name: your Russian ne'er-do-well name (German)

for Mrs. Jones

waking from a winter's sleep
the fire long gone out
the cold sharply pressing in on us
the dog and i

i hear the muffled sounds of my radio
and can almost make out the music
"The New World Symphony"
and the memory emerges slowly
as from the forests of another continent
before the plates shifted and some land bridge sunk into the sea

it was our favorite
to make love by—
the hours spent rocking
in passionate embrace
—a smile—your sweat—the fragrance of it
a few broken fragments . . . cries
how you said once . . . in some other lifetime
you'd been an old Japanese . . . man was it?
then we'd smoke a little again
become lost in a dream,
and finding each other then in this more profound trance
start over
like some Indian lovers on a frieze
blowing off the Kaliyuga—
the tender parts so delicately lyrical
as if morning had just broken on the prairie
and the exciting approaches and sorties
or just the twilit looks across the fields

in Spillville or southern Illinois
brought up always by our peculiar intensity
where we'd fuck till death do us part

Symphony from the New World #9
old Dvořák our kindred
sometimes we'd make the old motel in Olive Branch
shake with our love

but later when you were with others
you didn't seem to know how to be friends
you seemed to follow one con-man guru after the other
whether they were fucking you
or calling you a premie
and using your donations
for their twenty-mule team fleet of Rolls-Royces

the last time Charlie and i came around
on a circuit of the Midwest
we followed down the rutted clay road
where you'd lived with your lumberjack
and tried to raise your brood of children
the old strip mine on the other side of your place
causing the stream to run chemical red
the sign of leached-out life—
the door stood flapping in the wind
the house deserted
the neighbors said . . . "gone to California"
like the Joads i thought
"don't know where . . . just up and left"
Charlie found an old prescription in the barn
which had long since doctored your herd of goats
inside i found an old rebozo left behind

that had been yours for years
and took it for rememberance
now we're almost old
if you're still alive,
perhaps we become less judgmental
as the years pass
or rather the judgments we make seem to wash out
in some sense of the realization
of our not really knowing

your looks were already going
the last time i saw you
from hard mothering
and the fever you caught in Asia that ruined your eyes
you might even be a grandmother from little Willie
an old woman

i've lost track of your first husband my friend
and the second also my friend
is long since dead
everything scattered and lost
but that seems the way humans live
—to lose everything out of some carelessness
maybe it was inevitable
i hadn't thought of you with such sharp clarity
for years

how we were linked together by different ménages
networks of friends and lovers . . .
a crazy quiltwork of people turning in and out
until it all exploded
blew us into different worlds
not so much regret and loss, now at least
as just a touch of the old heat of our love and loving

the unique intimacy almost contained there in the memory of
    the music
and how in the woods just beyond the housing project
where you lived—one gray March day
—after we had gotten back together again
we swore to be lovers till the end
despite your being married
and i living with another woman
and so plighted our troth
in whatever scrambled way we could

that it didn't turn out that way
now seems fated by human strangeness and destiny
and leaves me with an old smile
a touch of bitterness, and wondering . . .

a spade a spade (grocery for the poor)

cut-rate goods for cut-rate people
you see more and more of them
come flooding in here in the last year or two
all the canned and packaged foodstuffs or products would you
    call them
stacked up on pallets
the smell of rank staleness hits you as you come in the door
as though poisoned bait gone sour—
in 90% of the stuff you surmise tremendous cholesterol levels
salt, sugar, saturated fat—
they line up without expression at the checkout
with their lumpy bodies, their grayish skin
the Mexicans from West Liberty
Orientals in the last wave of refugees from Southeast Asia
the Amish up from Kalona, some poor whites
and river rats from over on the Cedar
even a stray Indian or two
their carts jammed with white bread, frozen pizza
canned goods, sacks of white sugar, Campbell's Soup
Dinty Moore Beef Stew, sugar-frosted flakes of—
the little children wide-eyed
looking at all the different candies on the shelves and piled
    next to the register
"get this one, daddy" they urge with bated breath
a year ago they even had European chocolate
fifty cents for a bar of pure Swiss Milk
perhaps it was too good for this store
it soon disappeared forever
and then it was back to the cheaper crummier American brands
even the sacks of yellow onions which go for 59 cents
say something like "low-grade yellow onions"

as if we didn't know already
Sardines from Yugoslavia
Tuna from Thailand
Mackerel from Chile
bargains from the third world
from the exploited to the exploited
Marx would turn over in his grave
muttering in his sleep "from each . . . etc."
but then you hear it in your mind's ear like a bell tolling
"from each according to their ability . . . to each according to
     their need"
but here it's whatever they can squeeze out of you
and to each (of these at least) according to what trickles down
where do they all come from
you don't see them up around the university
they must be shacking up out in the boondocks
yet for the most part they seem quiet and reserved
as though circumstances had taught them their place in this
     world
probably considering themselves lucky
to have some shit-eating factory job or unemployment check
     for a while
now come to load up for the week
you'd think the Amish would know better
so many of them being farmers and such—
disheartening to see the black-bonneted, pale-faced, serious
     women
picking over what passes for food
in the back there are a few worn-out looking vegetables
sacks of potatoes, chemical carrots
and even a few half-reasonable grapefruit for cheap
the poor know that fresh, real vegetables are a luxury
probably for the most part beyond them

you imagine in your mind's eye the meals being cooked up
the white bread passed out with sugared peanut butter and jelly
    to sticky hands
all the rather slender children eating now for a while their so
    bright and tasty foods
drinking their Kool-Aid and eating their canned *frijoles*—
the older couples who have to make do on their social security
also here in line with the rest of us this evening
appearing rather subdued and anonymous
which way does your beard point tonight, Whitman?
are these the democratic vistas which have risen up around us
is this the freedom of choice they are always ballyhooing about
you see the beaten, pulverized look in their faces
as their eyes glaze over with blankness
and you wonder how long they will last
eating these rations, almost it would seem
designed for them—
the sort of stunned silence in which they wait
the few teenagers looking around furtively
the way they box up their goods themselves
with some mute satisfaction
then hurry on out to the car where they light up
drawing deep on death,
having cut a deal here for their week's grub
the bigger deal was cut long before
and against them
and now more and more we seem to have accepted it
as they have
as "human nature"
or acceptable indifference
or unstoppable greed
or just the small hard thing which is now life

who will smear lard on their faces
in a last beauty mask of death
who will throw potato chips into the open grave as they are
    lowered down
who will mourn their untimely deaths
establishing once and for all the reality of planned obsolescence

hasta la victoria siempre

will we be raised from the dead
as on judgment day
and ushered into the great hall of the people
and will we meet Che Guevara, Malatesta
Bakunin, and Rosa Luxemburg
who will have become the saints and martyrs
of the revolution
and they bestow their blessings on us . . .
and will we embrace old friends whom we had fallen out with
or lovers who had abandoned us long before
and what of our enemies
will we be finally reconciled
or will they be banished into a kind of hell
and will those slain in the struggle
or tortured to death
be made whole in some sense
or will they become part of the one great soul of justice and
equality?

hasta la victoria siempre
said as a kind of farewell
until then . . .
the faith must be kept
and the struggle continued
through various lifetimes
or incarnations, disillusionments
or alienations, losses, deaths, Stalinizations, freezes, and thaws
sleeps, rebirths, and enlightenments
and will the Buddha be there
to welcome us, or Christ?
will our mistakes, crimes, and lapses be forgiven and redeemed

will we dance with Vishnu, Kali, and the dervishes
in a last ecstasy of the soul's imagination
will there be a kind of Lord's Prayer for anarchists
that we will say each night in unison before we break bread
and will we have ceased eating the flesh of our fellow
    creatures,
heavenly and earthly,
in an ultimate vegetarianism

spoken as a kind of farewell
until then . . .

hasta la victoria siempre: until the final victory

"gray light awakening"

gray light awakening
just turned morning
black and white grain in the dimness
leaves out my upper window barely shift
still warm under the old torn covers
not yet public face
not yet cunning and exile
but only silence
yesterday put aside projects not yet gone awry
a brief opening along the gray margin
special moments
more yourself in these few
before the endless deflections
taken back to a sense of awakening with old loves
remember their pale faces
only just born out of existential dark
breakfast-making   sack lunches gatherings
work preparations of long gone times
your dog lies innocent and still curled in sleep
think of your aged parents
up even earlier than you
drinking coffee together in their own morning
tuning the news you hear again the many troubles of the
    world
and weigh as you can
the struggle between truth and falseness
on the day of my end
let me arise again in a space somewhat my own
and watch a last gray dawn come

so long it's been good to know you

cut out for the river on an October morn
find my friend Rick who lives in his truck by the railyard
the delicious smell of woodsmoke from the window of his panel
he's eating a fried tomato sandwich cooked on his oil-barrel stove
but feels sick today—speculates hesitating
on whether it's mono hep stomachache?
in a few days he might take off for Brownsville
and south Texas to pick citrus with the Mexicans
i walk over to the river and the ducks are quacking along the
    bank
calmly swimming and looking around
the wind comes over the trees
and there is a soughing deep-down
the tracks ripple off like silver snakes glistening in the sun
easy in the long thread of being dreaming
feet crunch in the cinder rock
glimpses of the river between the trees
its broad surface simmering in the October sun
the currents out there turning-as-they-go downriver almost past
settling into these moments
with a spirit of some luck
think of his face in the back of the smoke-blackened truck
half-pained, half-smiling, matted brown hair, himself

"winter"

winter
from across the road tumult of a schoolyard
circus of sounds, somersaults of pitch, circling
the diminuitive female—thrilling screams of joy
terrifying excitement,
young males bellowing   caught within the confines of a game
from your memory recess
they break out for a moment
a new crop taking root in the air
screams growing upside down like shoots of tender young corn
now silence, the presumed silence of learning
the cold air coming in my open window like a stream
then sleep a dipping downward
back, i come back from the dead
as i have before
with a disturbing sense that one day i will have ceased
to exist entirely
the expression muddier
until you are one with the dirt
is sleep a road
down which we advance carrying what?
those sounds—
unpleasant and frightening when you were a part of them
further and further from you now
take on a beauty
a purity that perhaps exists only in the imagination
a frailty that has no consciousness of its frailty
as from a moment in time they recede
down some road you are traveling
until only the thinnest hairsbreadth
of a glasslike and tiny scream

black November

pause on the railroad overpass
to see the rails rush away   by line of sight
to some far unknown
the straight hard industrial geometry
like lines of force move out from under me
. . . a bleakened beauty
the rails suggest that we too might move
with a straight strong force toward some chosen future
yet, the brakemen nose about in almost dark
like frail winter fireflies
and in back of that the town lies heaped up
a gothic rubbish pile
the trees so peculiarly black
against the smudged gray of the night sky
as i go walking by
and wonder if
whatever force be still left in me
will be sufficient to embark
upon a series of journeys
seeking a half-crazed lark which cries out now
and flutters confusedly
in the darkened roundhouse of my skull
as if by living as i do
thinking to gather my strength
it might be ebbing rather
as the streetlightmoonlight gives a phosphorescence
to a muddy alley down which i peer
feel the pull and undertow of strength and weakness
shift in my guts and teeter
and then go toward home resolving to wait
and work, test the wind

which blows down hard and indifferently in these years
try to trust the sap
in my own dark and hoary trunk
to bud, to wait for spring
or to tear the roots from this black earth
and go rootless walking
searching for a peachtime dogwood
whorl of world that like a strange dawning tide
might come in me, or to me, again

for Richard Hopper (died 1978)

spring finally comes though bitten with cold
the warmth loosens up my frozen insides
and suddenly i am crying
for all the terrible passage of things
of all the being born
and of the dying
of even the simplest things
the grass, the way a tree is
a room
and my weeping encompasses only a tiny piece
of all that is coming to pass
so much so that
for a few seconds
i grope to fathom how much
the whole of it
and especially the dying
to such an extent that
my weeping cannot grasp it
and i weep only my own poor sorrow
while trying
trying to grasp

"behind a large truck"

behind a large truck
spat out its muffler
it spews triumphant

over the winter bridge
the gray sky lowers
the dark iron of it
like a well-known gloomy face

the slightest whiff
of the right kind of diesel exhaust
puts me in Holland on a dark rainy November day
in Arnhem it is perhaps the same
it is as far and as strange
unequally the same

now in the wet wind i am years younger
put an innocent smile to the ruffled river
still as ignorant   the same confusion and hope

what next everything blowing
a dream that goes on until one day it ends and?
another begins?

here now over this machine only recently invented
but already ancient as futurist functionalism
i meditate on the vast ignorance of my life
many, many ignorances

i salute my friends whoever they are now
the beauty of man must be in some instinctual intelligence
some resistant hardihood of humor
for perhaps years hence i will come past this point again
to laugh and celebrate
the many-sided ignorances of my life

for Barbara

wandering the country roads in winter
the sky drops slowly into dusk
widths of darkness   cup the low sealike drifts of hills
snow like powdered sleep
white oblivion becoming a specked gray
drifts shift—blow toward "the apparition that swirls"
lose track of the road
in the midst reorient our sliding drifting machine

now brown weeds in the high beam's swath
whiskers on your grandfather's face
the stubble-colored rabbits of headlight fleeings
all asleep in their burrows
winter farms   a single outside light
illumines the silo face of the barn
a patch of the yard
as truly solitary as we imagine it to be

all our life one long sleep
death a friend come to wake us
hard to imagine that   sleep so thick in this waking dream
our little piece of musing ignorance   come creeping over the
        fields
this eiderdown of forgetfulness
my cock asleep in your hand
a snowbird dreaming the sleep of winter's peace
the caress of our thoughts mingling

over the dark streams that gave us birth and childhood
and beside which we might sit in the doddering of our bloom
far-off farmlights singly punctuate the distance
consciousness at its lit signal

black haystack house of death
lodge of our unknown ancestors
into which we will enter direct into darkness
grandfathers we are coming
carrying buckets of sleep up the hill of eternity
grandmothers, we wash our face in the black cream of night
and will come to you innocent of knowledge
sojourners, seawearyers
dead brothers and sisters
can you clue us in this long dark
can you hear these murmurings whisperings
can you feel the warm finger of our longing
probing your night sky

for César Vallejo
and his Profound Oxides of Sadness

take the broken ankles of consciousness
that wrench us
they still must push us on
from limping to straight speech
take out of our eyes the thousands of rifle sights
and one by one, dismantle
to make naked creatures
to turn these shoulders on a lathe
a great warm tongue of earth,
accept the small pebble Sisyphus gave us
and roll it on

the morning trembles with itself, with the future
even the sclerotic hardening of life quivers
concrete bunkers shake
for the joy of this wretched morning
coming on like a dim fluorescent light
ignorant of nearly everything, we scatter into chilly dawn

for Mike and Kim

quiet   light out the window
down the frozen river
swept with softly blowing snow
home again

light over the mountains fading down Sunday's decline
on the radio the lyric lilt of the vernacular
reunion at Folk City out of NYC

the roads again
the nameless communities sweeping past
"hear that long lonesome whistle blow"
some saxophone
pulling sweet melodies from the air

"laughter so light
it danced upon her breath
and lips from which it came a berry red"

dark creeping up the river
snow glowing in the shadows
with subdued intenseness
Odetta, "sometimes I wonder
do you ever think of me"

American despite myself
crazy fucked-up life
candle in the wind
shrug it off

"dust on your mouth
legends on your mind
sing me your sweet changes"

on down the road reading signs in the dark
cut by headlights   from a brutal mold—

desolate highways, past darkened commuter communities
as though they were all asleep
streetlights, isolate in their pools of light
sentinels—of a dead life—

sifting the lost fragments
that they not blink out
"sister help to trim the sail
Michael row the boat ashore"

Mike and Kim: friends, a couple, killed in head-on collision shortly before I
returned

"you feel the hollowness of being excluded"

you feel the hollowness of being excluded
no plans for you and the others
the unemployed, the homeless, the starving
the landless—
earmarked for destruction
—slowly you understand
you have to exist so the better-off can be kept in line
if they refuse to go along
they could end up like you
that fear must be instilled in them

the grain bobs in the wind, sunset colors the fields
we walk along knowing the earth is good

only among men
are we marked down not to survive
even the termites
even the insects
do not designate part of their number
to live outside the hill in little houses of grass

the hollowness gnaws away creating a nausea
we look at everything with a peculiar penetration
things are also hollow and gape open like a tomb

the elite ones speak and we listen to their words
we X-ray them with our hungry minds
and hear the crisscross of dishonest weaving
the music of hoarding
finally we understand—they cannot speak except to lie
we reap only the bitter harvest—the bitter knowledge

most of us will go under
but some will struggle and survive
will live to raise their swords and strike
then the powerful will weep crocodile tears
for the slain ones, will speak so reasonably
of the tragedy of bloodshed
while sharpening their weapons, remind us
that terrorism must be stamped out ruthlessly
but we will only shake our heads
shake our heads
—the waste, the uselessness
while at the same time thinking "i spit on your grave"

"dark men are speaking to dark men"

dark men are speaking to dark men
as though from the corners of their mouths
the sea fuming and gurgling, roaring like some kind of furnace
lead is sinking further in the marrow of their bones
some metal knowledge is speaking there
mortality is right if we could see it this way
like in some old photograph
they carry it in the dark folds of their overcoats
in the grime in the lines of their faces
in the hollow of their eye
i remember the convicts they did not care
one or the other they were constantly plotting
the enormous crime of their lives
to be done to them
or by them
muttering clandestinely to each other
the incestuous brutalities
which would be hammered from the air
but i to make pact with the trees
the night, the dark
with women or men enough strange
for the mutant river flowing over this cut shoulder

invincible summer

written while listening to Bartók's songs

returning from a swim
in the old stone quarry
walking in the road
to find myself in the central rut
feel the dark easy currents   flowing

tint of other cities
in the reflection of a diner's plate-glass window
63rd and Woodlawn at eight o'clock of a summer's eve
the same hunger of anonymous bodies
wandering in the summer sink, what could we do?

the last silver mica in the sky
last shining slate
as though on some auroral horizon
then six dusks mixed with the ink of night

in my memory of ancient summers
far-off swimmers take leave wordlessly
who have already taken leave
and now again
i hear the bump of strange oarlocks
the soft murk of their sloshing into water
as they begin the long swim

trees come up dark as signs
to be in one's body at last
moving easily through the soft evening

accept it all finally
even the most absurd, wretched—
to be so alone and content
a rareness

farewell swimmers, perhaps mine in some way
each for his own China

an evening then given over to solitude
take it for myself
in my room books speak to me
chthonic voices rising up from the earth
and this music close to the hub
radiating from the core
of some more intensely joyous and melancholy carousel
the wooden horses of my thoughts
drifting out toward the trees and hills

dusk . . .

the runners going from one to the other
in the uproar of families settling down
the sputtering of sparklerlike batons
amid the cries to the final darkness
towers struck full of stained light
or deeply knelling in the metallic sonorities
the somber falls   the towers falling
soundlessly against the moving sky
the day's hopes fading out one by one
the nightwatches beginning
among the lights on the other shore
the commingling of the incantatory gestures
exorcising light-dark dark-light
indecipherable dance of the semaphores,
on the sandbars going to and fro
death's stretcher-bearers stark and white,
the runners in the last agony of the race
the pewter philosophers savoring the dregs on their mugs

you and i
sitting under the blank wall of the sunset
warm shards of day in our bodies
listening for the last dusky cry in mulatto dark
muezzinlike
a trembling flute of hope   and resignation

night and the last fall
again the outcries calling out a final No!
from upriver the long wails of the river tugs
like an animal's muted bellowing
with the candlepower of their shoreward sweeping lights

piercing us crisscross and double-cross
pulling without end
barges loaded with our discontent
heaped high with the ore of sorrow
—somehow dimly a recognition
slowly moving abreast of us
winking blue and green
churning on downstream   for the confluence of two brown
   river-arms
rounding cape farewell
slipping out to sea drift

"how this morning"

how this morning
a few strokes moved me
how this morning
somewhere they say it is morning
the light seemed fake
yet i knew it was real
the burnt coffeepot a black ikon
here in this cave of wood
where i made a not-so-sacred fire
what moved me in the poem
threw everything up changed
the whole of it danced around me
as it had not for so long a time
while i grieved even in its beauty
for sadness sprouted everywhere
and even silence bent over her own breast
listening in sad expectancy

Luftpost (for Levy)

through the years
the slant deepens
on the bill worn by the postal employee
his face is now polished wood
his arms mahogany
he is bowed by our letters
one day we will have to deliver our own
all the way home
back through the countries where we were born
to those that gave us birth
although now they might be living ghosts
. . . and to those who slung us in the ditch
and these will sometimes be the same . . .
the letters washing off the page
and onto our skin
rising up through our mouths
strange fountain of stuttering
only becoming clear in our eyes
speaking their silences

for once to reach back and say it all
though it were only a handful of black blood
thrown in the face
or something strange called love
which even then will smile kindly
as though to say "you're forgiven
you didn't really mean it,
i know of the bitter canker
of the bitterest root of all . . ."

Luftpost: air mail (German)

for Judy

in the west day is drawn into the smelter of sunset
each grain of light and all it illumined
we might go out on the plain
weeping, crying out
protesting this loss
so absolute

instead there is the subdued silence of dusk
lights in windows burn stoically
with a sort of frail transcendence
as though an old woman lifted unsteadily
her withered arm
for a last gesture at day

a lake of dark comes washing up
stars put forth pale blossoms
what i loved
incinerated in a smoldering weeping

a cry
so far it is a wire scraping in the throat
of childhood's distance   filament of innocence

a house with cheerful yellow light
a woman wet with luscious peace
in the dark of her meditating eyes
who waits in quiet half-lit rooms

who turns
no longer waiting
and enters the smelter of night
the black factory

for my friend John
lying on the bed with morning heaves

"as of this date, you are being referred
to the SS *Henry Steinbrenner,* as a Porter"

cheap port
and muscatel day after day
his ex-wife tells me "I would live with him
if he could stop drinking"

met him at the courts   an old jock from the fifties
played a Cousy-like guard on dexies for Maryland
now he ships out on the Great Lakes
to sober himself on the sea
work up a stake for his family
and his binges

a Mick from Jersey
talks with that cocky East Coast bark
fought in the Korean War while still a teenager
when he sobers up a little we talk about Kerouac
calls him "Jack" as though he were
a strange lost brother

i hide his booze
but one way or another
he starts off and goes till passout time in evening
every morning then puking up blood followed by the dry heaves

he and his family are kaput
his screaming ex throws us out
for the last time;

ends up in Duluth on skid row
selling blood out of both arms the same morning
for a poorboy of wine

finally i cannot stand watching him commit suicide any longer
cannot stand his endless drunken harangues
against all the people who have ever abused him
against the government and the capitalists
even though most of what he says is true,
cannot stand his loud bullshitting while i am sick
and trying to sleep,
turn him into the street to live or die
at night he sleeps on the foam in the pole vaulter's pit
makes it to Chicago where his union dues are unpaid
haunts Christian men's association
sends word for money
i see his tormented face
against the background of the coldest city in the world

"Be advised, we have not been notified
of fit-out dates for this vessel."

"sometimes i want to take them in"

sometimes i want to take them in
those so finally estranged
who other times you cannot bear to look at
so remarkably like yourself do they seem

less good jammed in among the bad
and i wouldn't have made it
this far
among the survivors
to practice this strange art   of seeing things
on the still colored wallpaper

if only to understand one thing they have said
if only to forget oneself for one moment
and give them brief respite
down the long staggering road of their disintegration

to put my shoulder to some serious wheel
that i can almost see through a hole in the darkness

room in a penitentiary

down the dark Bardol corridors
faint murmurs . . . their spectral voices
beseeching . . . revenant
whispering voicelessly

a door is opened
the cell resembles Van Gogh's room
in Arles . . . the long solitary bed
the colors bandaged over
only the white shapes

the whiteness cuts
snowflake razors
the door is locked
i sit on the bed and weep
eyes swell open with prismatic tears
running color—into the remote void

brush strokes bleed snow into the clinical walls
at the sink   i cut off my mustache
it runs down my face
dissolving in the mirror into naked meat
as though i had no ear

i am only part Dutch
but i sit in his room
listening to the mute murmurous agony
spinning in the deep convulsive infinities

staring from the window
the sky shrunken to a patch
memorizing
remembering

Veronese green
wine red
maize yellow
crow black

the room is painting
a terrible self-portrait

a moment of sleep (for Schnu)

the gray light
on your sleeping morning face
simple, clear
like a road opening before me
the fog drifting away
an untroubled beginning

in sleep it almost regains
its unshaped origins . . .
framed by my glance
for these few seconds
hereafter never the same
folding in the bitter
and the good

each moment on the verge of waking
yet still, placid
sleeping the sleep of the ages
your face
in a moment of sleep
before time awakens us for its end

"stumble into the great red sunset"

stumble into the great red sunset
settling down over the river
which still goes on
even beautifully
carrying its silt and sadnesses
why not i in the same way

turned round and around by the twilight
the earth dazed and simmering
blink and look again
street cry humming into the song of supper
creatures thankful for one more meal
tacos and *frijoles*
water cold as some purity we cannot find anywhere

dusty rocks in my chest clicking
evening coming on without syntax or hope
still we philosophers of the boulevard of baggy pants
have one more tilt at the absurd
reheating the broth
savoring the sun's soup of days
before silence surrounds us

and the streets lead always
to other streets equally lost
nights along this wayfaring sadness
thinking this is how it will be in the end
some speechless gesturing
of awe and resignation

meditations on an old shoe

old shoe, like a dog who sleeps beside my bed
old brown hiker, soft red boot,
lie on your side, tongue lolling exhaustedly
the hole in your sole will soon be worn through
and you will be disemboweled, speechless friend

soft sloping leather shaped so wondrously
whose wrinkled road maps
are the history of my blood becoming earth

you have danced as dervishly as i could
the thump of the *fussball* in your square mug
strolled the fragrant flowers of foreign soil
and lain down beside a lover's bed
reminding us of our origins
when you lay beneath the blue-green lights of piney Christmas
before the ashen hearths of Chicago
the volcanic funnel of your boot top
beckoning a spelunker's sleep
making a poem of the soft woman i wanted
we have run off together

mute wanderer
you are dead leather
as i am dying leather

shoe, reminder of the worn self
and the ineffable tumult of shadow-fold reincarnatory
my thoughts wonder in silence

what would you say—all things are alive
even the inanimate?
let us arise and go now
into the soft hissing grass of morning

fussball: soccer ball (German)

for Han Shan on his Cold Mountain

sitting in the depths of this prison
counting the emptinesses
laugh that i could dream anything so absurd
then count them again
an infinite series

calm now, they cannot harm me with their schemes
occasionally they even let me read a few books,
in their outdated library i find Han Shan
how did you find your way to this most obscure of places?
it must have been a long and difficult journey

cold morning, cold stone
tomorrow perhaps i will know great fear
and even greater loneliness
what could it possibly signify?

i miss my old comrades
my books, hash pipe
and a woman
the last one
we almost touched

Han Shan, scarecrow of cold mountain
bag of bones laughing in the clouds
you give me heart
in the old age of my youth

"gentle as the Lamb of God made into mad cutlets"
—Lawrence Ferlinghetti

we go sailing on your breasts
which were like the sea
if you were to read this
you might wonder why   this body dreaming afterward

bodies carry a resonance of memory
long after the soul has fled
up its nightmaze streets
dropping the tattercraze sweets of soul-sweats
and top of the mountain blooming flowers of—
has gone
still bitter refuse of the most human ending
i have made with your ilk of creature
my ilk of creature?

it is bodies finally will tell the story
and if those rosebud breasts could speak?
a squeak of little-girl pink dreamlings?
and the brown tit of womanly nursings we squeezed
and so squirted in the ten different directions of space
illuminated milk tracers hung down curdling over the paradise
    trees
but when i tasted it, bitter and thin
as human love itself

it is bodies
the denatured brain must choose on the last auction block
might choose each other without hesitation
as each knows the other as part of that great flesh tree
will be washed up in the total animal soup of time

and in age
the thickenings
all the old droopings and sad hangings
caryatids growing too much flesh
to hold up the weight of the dumb ages
will speak, why did we hesitate?
why is it we held back and refused
and only now might know enough to give without stint
yet with sad foreknowledge of the incurled withered flower

we are loose in the red dreaming fields of evening
i am seeking you out over the snowfields of a winter's bed

summer evening

the dusk so thick, swarming, earthlike
that i can almost crumble it in my hands
break open this clod of magnetic fire
opening on a lone wandering
a turning down the corridor of years

the life of my heart   unwinds through my legs
i speak again with lovers long dead to me
my dogs arise from their graves to bark and run
twilight settles in my bones   a pale copperish dye
stained carmine with fevers and longing

yesterday i felt unbearable despair
today i wept copiously
this evening i am finally resolved
what could be simpler, what harder to fathom

workmen sit stunned on their stoops
the sky softly blesses
our ragged and pathetic attempts to find our way
supper is a bowl of warmed-over courage
a soup too thin   for the tasks of the morrow

the streets breathe the haze of evening
night creeps up from the hollows
darkness falls with an immeasurable softness
i search for a live face, a friendly body

the rhythm of pale shapes lures me on
into the green haze and the transfigured depths of half-light
birds settling in with a final cry of evensong

in the yellowish trailing sky
giving out on the last horizon
my hope and despair take form
a beckoning that burns away to a lingering green fire

in the dark
cold strangers
shoulder each other aside
i cannot understand
how they bear their own coldness

the sun now or never (for Barbara)

something spoke in the creek-ice
silence   far murmurs
as we walked along the river
so winding and small
naming it as you would a dog from your youth
we lay in the tawny marsh grass
out of the early March wind
which had no name not even March
the sun pulsed now or never
in a pure blinding Morse code
that tapped like fervent telegraphers in our wrists
it was enough that we lay together
our mouths grown very large
our tongues becoming exploratory creatures
nature nearly disappearing for a time
the crow with its rough cry
finally going up into the recesses of the sky
the plane overhead with its singing motor of man
thinning and growing so beautifully thin
with its faint palpitant drone
enough to be clean for a moment
and feel the bilge draining into the clear silence
to know that what you had left behind
was hardly worth returning to
the cluttered tangled life
drifting loose now in the meaningless wind
a song that has come to swoop you up

then in evening the long straight roads to the horizon
tiny towns we had never seen appearing suddenly
then disappearing, drifting specters of a prairie childhood

the vast sundown loneliness of those endless perspectives,
dust devils with a madness that resembles our own
clear sightings over the flatness of the land
a lifetime of knowing these roads;
driving through the past which slowly darkens
into the anxious evening search
for homebound lights
resting easy as the images melt into one another
to become a single rustling darkness

for Judy

our life splinters like the wood under my axe
i come down with all i've got
yellow- and white-grained logs fly off in great bitten chunks
wind tears at the sky   gales in the trees
desolate expanse of snow
mountains peaking up blue and celestially wild

wind rips at the chinks
with sound of prying nails from boards
downdraft in the stove   ghost spirits of the land
playing little humorous madness tricks
with Grandma's hair of stovepipe smokings
window throbs as though it were a crude tuning fork
fuck the spirits and their ancestors

our dog dead three months shot in the neck
lies up the valley
her grave covered with snow

American template
grizzled shadow darkening the continent
closing circle of life
axes falling on our gutted lives
some way out, some right choice
something to release from this anguish
meanwhile baling wire and bent nails
we go on, leave our blood in the snow

the gunmetal blue darkness of evening
silence hones in on the plane of the wind
the stove murmurs and shifts
look at each other in the dim kerosene light
"what are you thinking?"

dawn

a pure whiteness spreading
as though on a plain in Africa
slabbing, curling, whole trees of milky light
blooming slowly

i step out of my skin to be in this purity
such absoluteness
it enfolds other personal dawns of my own
in its long milk-white arms
encompasses all that i could ever be and beyond
dawns higher over my death
and the death of my friends
i smell the fragrance of woods and river in it
empties me of thoughts
and sets my prow straight into the white fiery mystery

slipping back into my skin
i think, it is enough
strange as it might have been
hard as it may have been . . .

seeing my small knowledge dissolve into the dawn
in one liquid movement
let it take me where it will

i sit in calm ignorance
watching the tides of light
carry us to an unknown shore

panhandle (for Annette)

i imagine it is not God that judges us
on this vast empty plain
but under the sky that does not end
and glimpsing the far reaches of the great plains
one stands more naked
exposed to some part of the core
thus does one judge oneself
painfully feeling the petrified wood at the center

etched on the landscapes of these realizations
the windmills made tiny by the distances
the abandoned houses in the small ruined towns
the Texans gaunt, desolated
drying up with the poverty
and meaninglessness of their movements
waiting tables in a chili diner   pumping gas
coming in from some remote acreage in a dusty pickup
under the peculiar washed-out gray of the sky
more dreary somehow than i can understand
all of it, distinct and barely wavering in the slow wind
the stunted trees in little groves
these withering beauties
this melancholy in the slow sad caress of the constant wind
a plainness that catches and confronts
holds me up to her words that sear with a slow sizzling truth
and to that inward sense that recognizes and confirms
gives way to some rarely reached feeling for a life's faults

rather than a mingling and breathing with
—the hard give-and-take of offense and forgiveness
some understanding and identified sharing

—to have feared, suspected, and judged
yet i ask myself how could it have been otherwise
with those that i still cannot forgive, fathom
survive with
yet despite this, her accusation is true
judging from the corner you've been forced into
to judge as harshly as the prison
they would have you inhabit
yet this an admission of the inability to free yourself
stand clear
instead   judge them all fiercely   and her

Amarillo a blur of lights
towns beaded along the road
already dropped off into a desolate darkness

beyond our needle of light, opening out
in the huge black spaces of the plains night
these questions finally subside and drift off
a lessening of painful thoughts
plowed under in the dark by a need to forget, go on, and live

the few, scattered lights
remote harbingers of other
chances, to inhabit, kindle, accept
this strange life
its possible beings

rising up

rising in the stained, gloomy dawn
sodden and corroded with the history . . .
with the murders, exploitations
as though the traffic spoke of it
growled it out under its breath
passing its heavy baton on to you, the individual
of poverty, humiliation, prison
its agony like a foreknowledge and an aftertaste
a writhing thread in the flux of things
and the shape of things to come

rising up morning after morning
which way do you turn
which brother do you try to convince
of something he already knows in his bones
—to what remnant of hope
which words express
—speak them to whom?

hookah

still haunted
   by the hookahs
      of old cities

billowing fogs
    blue with irreality

roller coaster of epiphany and memory loss

dingy back stoops
   where i slip in from the mists
           unnoticed

shadows of mysterian Doctor Sax
   dancing up the dark twisted stairway
     burst into the red attic
   aromata of pungencies
     mosques floating in the smoke-drifted ceiling
music hanging on lascivious smiles
         like languid butterflies
   eyes liquid embers dark dreamy coals
    fantasia of my very own creatures

gravity disconnected
   we float in our warm-hued chambers
    far beyond the bleak balustrades

when they come for us
   perhaps it will be a dark funeral coach
    drawn by six blind horses

and we'll hear, like the tinkling of a bell
the fatal flawed laughter
of a yellow cracked buddha

still haunted
far beyond
the bleak balustrades

down the lanes and paths (for Stack)

running again
through the woods
and up the hills,
finding a stride
a way through the brush
and up the inclines
though not as lithe as before,
running from old sorrow and old crimes
in the silent woods
only the tick of the rain
the ciné movement of a squirrel
each abrupt movement ending discontinuously
minding his own business in the leaves

weeping through the trees
as the breath breaks open
releasing the sadnesses
that are beaten into you
and creep into your bones

picking it up down the hills
letting it out
lunging down the path
until you are afraid of falling
running to, and running from . . .
until you think—nothing to run toward . . .
so we are running away
through the streets and across the avenues
cutting through the vacant lots
past the piles of trash
and all those still asleep in their holes

still dead to the world
—now up the steepnesses
hunching into it
slowing, slowing near the top
until you must look like
a strange old man almost running in place

down to the creek now flooded
where the ducks cruise in flotilla
over the dam they built ruining the wild park

finding an old stride
that hasn't given out
some pickup in the old ass end
steadying now on a reserve
that suffuses a warmth

running out from towns and cities
along the gravel roads and blacktops
eye caught on the horizon, grove of trees
old farmhouse, some shining distance
with that illusion
that you could go on forever
nothing to break your stride

remembering years before
you and your old running partner that fall morning
fields covered with hoarfrost
you jumped the fence—deviating from the route
out across the fields shouting and laughing
freed, and across the next
not caring how far you went
or where you ended up

down the furrows
through the corn
jumping the streams or splashing through them
one day when you ran free

now the rain beads harder
the footing more treacherous
as you come down the last hill
. . . catching your breath
as you stand under the picnic pavilion
you notice some soggy paper plates almost submerged in a
    puddle
discolored with food stains and near dissolution
. . . and you wonder
how long does the breath hold out?
how far must these legs carry you?
away into the world
through it and still further

ensamhet

when even to withhold
one's being overtired of certain things
seems a distance, a turning away
thus a suffering for the other—

i remember a dream i had as a child
i had to walk down a road paved with faces
with noses up sniffing, eyes that saw
mouths that cried out and accused

i wished desperately not to trod
stood transfixed without stepping
like a stork with one leg drawn up in the mind
but something compelled me
what—i did not know
and so i went, gingerly, awkwardly
quaking with each step
walking on those faces
hearing the gasps, feeling the winces
the road seemed to undulate with writhing
this suffering—a net thrown down on us from all sides
twisting and struggling—as it tightens
we the trapped beasts
yet the worse for knowing—
the distinctions and possibilities
between those deliberately chosen
and those inadvertent
how they intermingle and rearrange
then recombine to make the fabric of our entrapment
and those who feign helplessness to do otherwise
with their mocking pity and sterile excuses
that pass in a dead world

there are moments
when one swears
never to be the hunter
and less often the hunted—by some clear seeing
never clearly enough
hunter and hunted
in a dream called by many names

ensamhet: loneliness (Swedish)

mixed signals

from my propped radio
the long anguished fall of the violin
then a tense silence, poised and fraught
perhaps something by Hindemith or Berg
and again crying there somberly
alive and darkly sonorous on the air

in back of that more faintly another station
the blues harmonica along some red-dirt Southern road
a tormented black singing
"since my baby done left me . . .
i gave all this daddy had
she caint do nothin
but treat me bad
stop being a fool for her
she carry on down the road
and i caint help
caint help feeling sad"
—the two modes inextricably bound up
a certain asymmetric symmetry

the music of our forking paths
already implicit in our horizons
still something of us must travel those other roads with them
and suffer also their almost singular fates
impossible—yet the broken imagination
struggles on with the spilled guts
dogging shadows of those we loved

or being with those who live in tales
there also an existence
might we ourselves live in a story written by God

even passersby in the streets
to follow them into what must be their homes
and watch their hesitant gestures
listening to their caught breathing
as they make their shattered love
take note as they struggle for breath
and their hands clutch their throats

now a swelling
as though the winds rose darkly in the forest
and ominous gathering and encirclement
Sibelius or Dvořák
delicate foreshadowings which foretell our lives
strung into a music of the soul

i search down the band in my solitude
as though one might actually hear a human voice speaking truly
a distant signal giving witness . . .
instead a preacher who ejaculates his despair
whines and implores, threatens and castigates
"whosoever believeth in me . . ."
he would have us send money for his special prayer cloth
but the station weakens . . .
the hysterical and power-hungry voice grows fainter
his all-too-human voice diminishing
until tiny words rave on—a fragmented crackling

then static like some cosmic rain
that falls in the gutters of time—without relief
and a long silence
patterning into dust

harvesters

they come together for a time
camping in tents, trailers,
bunkhouses, shacks, tepees,
raking blueberries outside of Machias
or Cherryfield on the barrens
picking up spuds around Presque Isle
detasseling corn in Iowa
tobacco in the sandy loam of southern Ontario
picking tomatoes in western Ohio for the canneries
pruning the suckers from apple trees in Vermont
climbing the ladders
crawling the ground for drops
then it's over
"goin' to Yuma for the winter, for lettuce"
or planting trees in Louisiana and Mississippi
watching over their shoulders for the corporate inspectors
while illegally cutting the roots, sending the warning yip
schmu—ou!
bringing down their hodads with a thump
making the holes for the baby loblollies
their motto "we plant tight and deep"
some have names like Coyote, Indian Pete, Rhode Island Jim,
Tall Dale, Big Man, Corn Woman,
or plainer ones, Mary, Tom Fu, Manuel Gutierrez, Arkansas Sue
old women and young boys
squatting side by side in their stooping labors
brown and white, Indian and swart
in this world they are regarded as nearly
the lowest of the low
no one asks why they have come
or where they are going

sometimes when they are in the trees
airplanes come over spraying ethylene to hasten ripening
but it's too soon and several days later
the planes come spraying "dontdrop"
they are expected not to complain
they are expendable
the pesticides lodge in their bodies
they wear out in middle age
from hard work and poor conditions
but they know the harvest
it is bred in them and grows in their bones
the feel of the earth
the scent of its bouquet
the satisfied tiredness in the sunset
that says so many bins today
the simple suppers around the campfires
the whoops of wild drunkenness
at their parties under the harvest moon
the brief friendships of the summer
flare up in them magically
and the sorely tired ones of long treks
and work wanderings
wear like the old leather of their shoes
i who sojourned among them
marvel at these still nomadic tribes
broken into atoms or little familial bits
these "hunters and gatherers" who must gather for others
and take the smallest portion for themselves
whose hunting becomes hunting for work
in the late autumn when others are battening the hatches
they disperse like leaves in the wind
where do they go?
do they take other guises

unemployed factory labor, tramps
their browned faces slip unnoticed
into the anonymous crowds
harvesters, still capable of beating the old tom-toms
still knowing some primal source
others have abandoned
weary in their old worn vehicles
looking with their quiet eyes
over the steering wheels and down the roads
they estimate silently
the distance they still must travel

"to be against . . ."

to be against   to resist everything
to plant yourself against their juggernauts
and nick off what you can
to use the resources which they have stolen from all of us
against them
to thwart them consistently in whatever small ways
to spread rebellion in the byways
fanning it like some small match fire
two leaves burning brownly together
this some resolve which you feel now strongly
but which tomorrow will waver
and almost disappear
a revolutionary consciousness to be attained
how far from really being, actually existing in you
how difficult to communicate this to even one other human
    being
and to keep in mind when again and again necessity forces us
to pursue some diversionary tactic in order to get by
how this too might be used to strengthen our own resources
and always against them

to survive—which for us is to resist
to take up our part in this long process
which sometimes goes so slowly
and with so many setbacks
that we think it is not really occurring

but we are edging forward
as though part of a wave of consciousness
eroding the oppressive shores

what would the Buddha say of all this
perhaps just to laugh gently and grant us
the intensity of our belief

how disappointing this isolate life
in which we are so alien from the many
we have grown so strange we hardly recognize one another
—as human beings?

one does not know, i do not know
and always it seems beginning again
taking a first step

for Barbara

crawling out from under the hedgerow
past the old rusted implement—harrow or?
through the stickery weeds and over the little creek
back up the dirt road that cuts through the corn
i wondered if my ancestors had done it the same
the men pulling up their trousers
the women smoothing down their dresses
better off for having done it among the elderberries
smelling the acrid dust of the gravel roads
then perhaps just mud
the straight roads intersecting a geometry of the imagination
that follows rise after rise on the prairie sea
listening off sharply in the distance
and maybe only hearing the faint rustle
of the wind in the corn
and the hum of the telephone wires
picking up a bit of dust by the roadside
stopping there to look, sifting
the September sun and the corn going brown
our intent wondering
what it might have been
the silent men getting into the buggies or Model Ts
the women coming up behind
picking their way through the underbrush
what were they thinking?

that they'd done what seemed most natural
and whatever the outcome
they'd remember this day, or others like it
all the places they'd left their seed
their passionate forays or lackadaisical slippings

those that gave them what they needed for a moment
maybe they laughed as we did
realizing we'd returned to our origins without thinking twice
entered the earth again through the wigwam of smoke sleep

had our ashes hauled, as it's said
and strangely i thought of my father taking out the clunkers
from our old stove in the coal bucket
whatever else it meant slipping away from us
so we could smile our sad animal smiles
somewhat bereft of illusions
and think back on those who must have also done it thus
and become aunts and uncles and grandmas
spoke no more about it
except to muse occasionally in certain Indian summer light
as though to themselves and secretly

you'd have to take these backroads for hundreds of miles
and into the night, cross the river into the dawn
for hundreds more and into the twilight
to find the remnants of their old farms
with broken pumps on cracked wells, newspaper for insulation
between the joists, the old pathetic implements gone to junk
in the crumbling sheds
a spavined shoe in an upstairs room
and then out to the cemetery to see what's become of them
the white-lime cementlike stones
now so frailly carved
just the names with the years and "his wife Marie"

as we cross the river the sky goes on illimitably
such that we might think one day there'll be room for us
in that big blue field

just as well join that vast hoedown
that's going on just beyond our reach
there Grandpa will no longer be crotchety and severe
nor Aunt Bess ruined and crazy
all your brothers and sisters
who died as they tried to be born
will be there dancing a crazy Irish jig
the music won't stop nor the cider keep coming

—if there is such a place
we'll lie down with each other again
in the grass and weeds
and do one of the few things
we know properly how to do

for Schnu

my dog woman
my cat woman
bear woman
times we were like prairie dogs playing in the grass
like wolf mates on the tundra
kitten woman
my otter woman
we might have lived imprisoned on the factory farm
pecked each other to death out of rage and frustration
as we teetered on the chicken wire in our cubicles
perhaps for our wildness they caught us in the steel-jaw trap
and we had to gnaw off our legs to escape
maybe we are of the strange species
Nietzsche called "the sick animal"
my goat woman
brown bison woman
my laughing white-fish woman
now our spawning is swimming up different rivers
we are migrating toward different poles

in the preserves rhinos are poached and left to rot
only their horns are taken to be ground into aphrodisiacs
in the labs Copenhagen rats are bred to have genetic tumors
half again the size of their bodies
the electrodes are planted in the heads of monkeys
into the eyes of rabbits are delicately eye-dropped toxic
     cosmetics
in the oceans porpoises are thinking strange thoughts
and must have already reached their conclusions

in the towns the dog fascists are rounding up suspects
to be vivisected and battered to death
in the most grotesque experiments

she watches over them
suffers for them
this hyena woman
with the tender hyena face

the elephants remember
as they are being killed for their tusks
somewhere a species is extinct and i am a part of them
in my dream a litter of mice was aborted
their pink naked bodies came hemorrhaging forth bloody and
    dying
i cried out for her to help
but she could not reach to me
these were our children

now in the evening the animals are silent
and grow sad with each other
the mammalian grief tints darker
my lynx woman
my coyote partner
with whom i have scavenged at the edge of cities

on the plains
the last wild horses are run down
to be shipped to the pet-food factories
and put into cans
the earth's last mustangs
their eyes desperate in the sunset

my dog woman
my orphan girl
my feral companion

Free Clinic

the basement of a church
one fan slowly circling from the ceiling as in an old-time
    drugstore
a shabby clientele of exposed flesh swelters on this July night
yet we rest easy with each other
some maybe knocked up, or with the clap
a urinary-vaginal clog-up, or needing birth control
a constant parade of people to the john
with their paper cups to get the clean-catch in its free fall
a kid acts up, his ma dupes neither him nor us
with her candied "come here I have something to tell you"
when she grabs ahold of him she tells him alright
in a staccato of threatening whispers

"does your stream split?
do you dribble a little more?
when was the last time you were treated for venereal disease?"
old John asks then practices his blood pressures on me
i tell him then, i'm just now trying to get it down too,
this sphygmomanometer
i sit without a shirt, it fell in a puddle in the examining room
and meet some young guy
lank and intense
he tells me he takes medication for his anger
you can tell he's a little proud of it, this anger
"I get very military when I get mad"
this crack shot talks of M-30s, shooting the tops of bottles off
at a hundred yards, maybe going after Reagan
and how a girl got angry at him once
he felt sorry for her, knowing that she might provoke him
to some dangerous point

and what he might do (this last bit he recalls with juicy would-
    have-been anticipation)
he's latched on to some little hillbilly girl from South Caroline
bright as agate her eyes, you could spot her instantaneous
in a lineup of these bigger Northern women
a little crooked somehow she is, ass bulges out
slightly bowed in the legs
and talks along with her man
a kind of vaguely threatening sweet hillbilly insistence
she's curious about me, looks me straight in the eye
as none of the others would
something subhuman they might judge her
yet she stands out   a more intense animal presence
some part of an old soul or body they haven't knocked out of her
    yet
she could only get a dollar-something an hour in 1981 in South
    Caroline
after she graduated from high school,
so she came North where now she can vie for minimum wage
i overhear her tell her patient advocate that she's missed her last
    period
she'll begin her brood of young groundhogs, chippy monks
fighting hillbillies
maybe they won't take pills for their anger
but point it straight and make it stick

the medical student says cough, with his finger up my scrotum
feels up my ass with his gloved probe
he and John go over every possible angle of my trouble

in the end i'm waiting again without my shirt
remembering through the yellowing wallpaper years
most that i know end up here

on the edge of their rickety wood-slat chairs
waiting for children, prenatal care, fatherhood
abortion referral, prognosis, pills
some cure or cure-all
grand central of the disenfranchised and malnourished

it strikes me in a strange lapsed conclusion
that these others here are actually trying to give us aid
some kindness bestowed, care apportioned
patients' rights tacked up on the wall
no hotshot medics here

the student pharmacist gives me my free prescription
and i go out into the sultry night
thinking of the vague anxiety in the women's faces
and imagine all the people lying up in their rooms
sweating, trying to fuck, oozing
drinking too much, getting high, listening to their children cry
wondering where their next whatever is coming from

lighted windows (for Judy)

Walk the night-scented streets
looking always in lighted windows
hoping for a glimpse of what shines out
marking the shades of yellow
faded   homelike
the color a kind of intimate perception,
refuge for an unknown being,
shading my memories of other nights
other rooms

till coming on the remembrance of you and me
roaming the streets
one early autumn evening   after smoking

and recall the flaring promise of lighted windows
intense curiosity roused to torch-flame
for the genius—beauty
the loneliness, common fare
the complex presences
that might be seen there
the evening star risen to the second story

yet what we saw
bore so little
of what we hoped for
as though that lit-transparency
opened on a dark opaqueness
that separates us all
so profoundly
as you and I become
slowly in the rumbling

of the years
more difficult to decipher
each for each

but as I walk
in this thaw-warm night, deep into autumn
that promise flares in me again, and standing
on the railroad overpass
while a train
rumbles gigantically underneath
the worn-gray city offers up its lights
and bits of lighted windows
—what's left of stars
strewn and shattered   yet nestling
in the hazy tattered leavings of the years

"when you live in your car"

when you live in your car
rather than a room
you get up more slowly in the morning
waiting and watching for the warm light to strike
roll out of the slightly cramped position,
and the morning blossoms
a waste field full of dandelions;
the bushes along a tiny creek will do for trees
having branches and leaves
and even the blank wall of the closed-down factory
we furtively parked behind
has its Zen-like associations
a flood of memories
something you were then
which now you can smile at, accept . . .

not having a roof, a ceiling for thoughts
and getting things going while she sleeps
you sit on the hood of the car
and your mind slowly opens to the extent of the sky
its striations, great masses of low clouds . . .
sounds and shapes seem more distinct
the singing of the highway in the distance
someone drops a tool, it clangs on the concrete
a delicate hammering with its high-pitched chink-chinking
a crow comes over the roof
with a disconsolate cry   piercing and full of curses
you scare each other when he first sees you
and flies limping off with a few choice words

you remember an evening in northern Ontario
after the long empty stretches had passed
with nothing but thick taiga on both sides
a moose that paused at the edge of the woods
then disappeared

Arctic watershed beginning just to the north
then a few fields again, farms
through French-speaking towns
where the French and Indians coexist
sometimes looking both so bleak and distraught
there was a strange monument along the road further on
you pulled off to see . . .
scuplted man, woman, and child
holding hands atop a stone pedestal

"In the early morning of Aug. 4, 1963
not far from here 3 members of the Lumber and Sawmill
    Workers Union
were killed as well as 7 other wounded
in order to saveguard the rights
of organized labor everywhere."
we stood struck—
the prairie wind fingered our hair
the silence breathed very slowly
—then not at all

"This is to the memory of Joseph Fortier
born 1928, Irenee Fortier
born 1938"
and one more
brother and sister? husband and wife?
or from the same clan
and one whose name you forgot

were they mostly French caught in some ethnic poverty
or had they, crossing lines, joined with some others—
immigrants perhaps, to struggle fraternally . . .
but the inscription in English? for us maybe
as though to say, we'll tell you in the way you'll best understand

you imagine sighting down the rifles of the Mounties
or the company men—the instant after they fired
into the crowd of unarmed strikers
as though from there,
seeing the cruelty of it straight on—the crimson splotches
the bloody tableau as though fixed in time
and then like a film that starts up again the cries
the fearful moaning, the agony of the bodies strewn out

the 10 P.M. sun cast its bright luminous Arctic glow
the black flies bit us on the neck and back of the head
they swarmed over the dogs
we walked back through the little woods
and looked at the abandoned shacks
hardly anything left—
put in a liter of oil and started off

the mornings come slowly
and more simply   if you're lucky
and other times estranged, claustrophobic, and lost
your friend still asleep in the back
you see over the fields to the lake
the mist rising slowly
something straightens in you and reaches out
does justice begin then in fragmentary glimpses
of things barely imagined?
but will-o'-the-wisp you wonder—and it's gone

from Oslo

blue dark of early morn
electric tram-flash in the "sail" of small nosing *sporvogn*
in first streakings from an overpass a railyard's great circuitry
    of steel
slender symmetry of taut design fanning out
touched against the dark wood and worn metal a light powder
    frosting of snow
cindered patches shadowed bluish
behind which city's red-brown
svart-gray of slow mornings coming

in fjord boats moving out
huge ferry engorges itself with train cars
fjord seeming to open open its harbor arms to the sea

leaving from under the overhang in Ost Stasjon
opening out to mountains ringing the city
sprinkled with twinkling lights of early morning risings *frukost*
    preparations

through slumbering trainyard dark rusted boxcars dozers
    dreamers
sea arm of harbor touches near
in the grayed light boats stowing holds with careful winch liftings

now forest of birch conifers
fields engraved with snow
small lakes summer cottage shored
gray fields under black and white clouded morning
intimate glimpses of close-packed spruce

high metalscrape of wheels against rail
screech of brakes
then up-tempo
past rail crossing with waiting bus strange swaybacked caterpillar

snow caked through pale brown weeds or lying in switchyards
as though left over refuse sublime into gray chiseled patterns

or hieroglyphed through open fields
abstract expressionist indecipherable script

stopped in some concentric moment hearing the "ready" whistle
of *en norsk* conductor careful-eyed checker of minute *tidtabell*
    seconds
laggardly *inngang*ers *ut*goers

passengers quietly reading their *dagbladets skandalblaska*
or sleeping *sova dormir schlafen*
dim to journey's shapings deadheading back

through echoing ravine of scarped rock
down-flow of frozen rivulets
sudden fjord opening placid water stretching to opposing
    small hills

in the east a pink rising over small *ö* of rock becoming white-
    orange
fields with immense fertile-seeming depths laid open
    ploughed in preparation
flowing out to thin sharp *kirke* towers against the dawn
green patches—lakes of snow
birds on their way now turning as if—abrupt angle of shifted
    bearings

power lines with ceramic holders turned down in semaphoric
    gesture
gradually rising and falling merging of cleffed rhythms

mysterious forests standing quietly as though in their stillness
preserving their virgin core

cars along a road tiny insect traffic with human aphid chauffeurs
more gray ploughed fields turned over to their ancient earth
    patterns

feather-tipped Indian arrows of roadbedside weedgrains
    tan-staunch
standing close up
hollow clank-echo of passing over bridge
mush-frozen bog pond cattails for breakfast

cranes standing in harbor isolate aloof all skewed differently
alienated citizens of their own measure

great hill-standing-highup-lookingdown houses
reklame of sliced tomato   arcing of bridge over water
red snowroof-laden boxcars

on tilted hills apple trees in autumn's gray gnarled twistings
bent natural and would-be fruited

old *svensk* brick mansard-roofed 19th-century house
first manor house, then poor farm, orphanage, cut into flats

smokestacks trailing smoke over near breadth of horizon
low hazy drift of horizontally framed lives

backs of houses as train cuts through
tired gutted factories pitted with dark
rusted freighter alongside, deck packed with cargo
now council flats five *vaningar* high one after another in estate
    pattern

man with sharp red beard greets his small *pojke* at station
picks him up tenderly
kysser his *kvinna*, stands expectantly poised beginning to turn
stern thin-sharp whistle blows small martinet bird
*dirigent*ing whole trains
slicing scenes with arbitrary time frames
barely noticeable jerk and almost imperceptible roll forward

industrial froth downriver from dam—sucked into rapids
blackbirds dip down in fields
land next to iced-over misplaced rut
from car or wagon two feet long
a natural for checking *sykkel* flats—break the ice

dawn rising higher over mountain ridge
lastbil in the distance truncated automotive bulldog
and i somewhat clear seeing somewhat unattached
with sadness let go of
almost content with what so irretrievably exists
real beautiful absurd multiformulous and slipaway

logs jamming a river floated down from the north
sun slanting down fjord
boring through tunnel of utter dark
seeing face of older self in window

clouds breaking
steep mountain passage over valley far below
autumn withering of deciduous
so many journeys packed so densely inside

light on pale pink-white of birchbark glistening
snow a steady glow of tender white
clouds reforming solid swirled phalanx—
little weeds quivering in the face of the windsbreath
juletre limbs laden with snow
over beds of ferns delicate brown grasses lightest snow layings
great frost architecture and articulation of dense forest's bed

small red railroad cottage at edge of woods for tools, lanterns
in days dream of night passage
finding lodging there with unknown companion
sun glaring off ice blinding beautifully

then see through ice-skimmed forest
all illusion, no wisdom here

only passage
only a moment of clarity
as we move through fields to our destination
a rare straight cut of perceptions
in the muddy muddled stream of time
clearly doubts fears arising from other spans
striking through to present
where among humans do i go
jumbled in our mismatched unfathomable intentions
in our crazed geographies of use, ownership

now boats thread the narrow channel of the Göta Älv
gigantic towering bridge to industrial suburbs, landfills
approaching the trainyard at Göteborg (Yutabory)
twisting snake yard of rails quivery
amid the multiple confusions of signal grids
the train brakes—and slows—to human walking proportions
as though in a strange last drift
cracked laugh and sly expression of one passenger to another

as if emerging from journey's dormancy
long last *stad*-gray day of strangers
milling though errand-bound
seeking, but concealing, masking
shorn—but of a stump
of human aspiration and intention
there in the dim *svensk* winter *lys*
through the lens of the window
faces inscrutable to me

sporvogn: streetcar (Norwegian)
svart: black (Swedish)
frukost: breakfast (Swedish)
en norsk: Norwegian (Norwegian)
tidtabell: timetable (Swedish)
inngang: entrance (Norwegian)
ut: out (Norwegian)
dagbladet: newspaper equivalent to *The National Enquirer* (Norwegian)
skandalblaska: scandal rag (Norwegian)
sova: sleep (Swedish)
dormir: sleep (French)
schlafen: sleep (German)
ö: island (Swedish)
kirke: church (Norwegian)
reklame: advertisement (Norwegian)
svensk: Swedish (Norwegian)
vaningar: floors (Swedish)
pojke: boy (Swedish)
kysser: kiss (Swedish)
kvinna: woman (Swedish)
dirigent: direct (Norwegian)
sykkel: bicycle (Norwegian)
lastbil: truck (Swedish)
juletre: Christmas tree (Norwegian)
älv: river (Swedish)
stad: city (Swedish)
lys: light (Norwegian)

Kattegat

the gray miles that go off into the distance
until mist dims them to invisibility
out there in the far remove i see phantom coasts   hulks

the sea flashing far out its white manes
like fish of ice that appear and disappear

close in the running wake a brilliant moving frost
traces of vomit on the upper deck
a single solitary seagull breasting the wind, tacking deftly
trailing sentinel of another way

at the edge of the horizon   remote possibility
small boat or fishing trawler
keeps its distance   unreachable speck

through the mist a thread of silence
marking whomsoever—

the coasts of our going—shores of the silent
as though struck dumb in the long haul of time
or sadder wiser than i know
yet the fine rain on my face
some possibility of a life touching
the moan of the wind   the lifeboats overhead
reminding

or only for me
or in me now, the silence

148

then real coasts
rise of land
slender tower
and wondering in the dim day's dawning
where something is headed
how far it would take us
where someone will disembark

Kattegat: a part of the North Sea west of Sweden, south of Norway, north and east of Denmark.

"stumbling and weeping"

stumbling and weeping
under the late night paper trees
gasping for each breath
en gammel svensk rolling in his autumn overcoat
en gubbe utan sin gumma
loneliness, the unbearable plague
mixed with the poor cure alcohol
ascribing to him something of my own obsessive plight
seeping through the years
marking us like a pox
some deep fissure that cracks our being,
none count the deaths, nor stack the dead
but in the mornings one sees the muddy faces
groping for the light
having left something of themselves behind

the silence stiffens   the inner gnarling twists up
like rheumatism's hands in pain
and what we know of this
cakes our faces like a slowly growing rust

en gammel svensk: an old Swede (Swedish)
en gubbe utan sin gumma: an old man without his old woman (Swedish)

distance between us

in a corner are the young women
spirited and free
through the din and smoke
you can see them talking with their knowing smiles
but you only hear a fragment here or there
your memory goes back and you think of Russian factory girls
outside Archangel or Smolensk
singing some obscene provocative song
. . . of my first . . . a Yugoslav
and how when we left the *bier stube*
we grabbed hold of each other in the dark
slipped to the ground and went at it
our tongues slithering back and forth
and the one gets up now who reminds me
she can't keep her feet quiet you see
the music is like a temperature
that makes her molecules bounce
and whatever else you could say of her
she's not a bourgeois
i look at her with a mixture of desire and indifference
but mostly indifference
whatever is left of our sexual life
of our coupling
is like a garden overgrown with weeds
we'll never experience the half of it
whether of delicacy or passion
and most less than that
i look at them again as i and my drunken friend get up to leave
. . . best to have no regrets
realize a secret of this life
is finally not to care

for all the friends you could have made
had you and the others been able to talk
and all the ones you could have been with
had there not been some terrible fear twisted into things
and a grotesque contempt the one for the other
when we die i'm sure we won't even think of it
only this strange thin strand we call our life
which by then will be even more isolated
from the complex and estranged fabric of being
and from what might have been still remotely possible
and the possibilities you once saw
for some open and free affection
will seem like foolish childlike dreams
—it will be a rag tied to a bush
in a forest where nothing comes
or some long-distance wire
strung into the woods of the Northwest Territory
at the end of which from some tin-can telephone
our voice will be heard by no one
saying Hello, Hello, Hello?

bier stube: tavern (German)

for Dr. Dewey

a few days come your way
a few free days
as winter is ending
and you begin to collect yourself
you have time to read, begin to exercise again
to get a grip on your body
in the mornings you go back to bed around 7:30
and wake up a little later remembering in the pale winter light
and certain of these memories come into a focus
you understand them in a way that hadn't come to you before
one day you go visit an old lady, a doctor
she tells you she's almost lived
her three score and ten
and that anything beyond that will be a bonus
something about her rough skepticism
her railing against the current dark decades
that gives you a feeling
your kind are cut off
from most of the older generation
but here you sense a link, a connecting thread
someone out on the headlands
about to begin a journey we know so little about
you remember how she tried to get you through certain
    sicknesses
and now you both still walk the earth

one day you'll be an old duffer, if you live that long
and how will you
help them live

the poets

as though they were minting crisp new words
like the colored currency of some fabulous new country
with peacocks and liberators on horseback
on some greenish-purple backdrop,
suggesting a treasure hunt—hints scattered in a pattern
zeroing in from some new oblique perspective
as if . . . could we see it from the correct "acute" angle
a straight shot through the fragmented barriers,
or they think it is in the flash of the bevel
the intricacy of the evasions
coyly hinting and alluding—backing away and then dancing
    forward
like mental patients (in what asylum?)
who can't afford not to speak schizophrenese
or like bureaucrats (are they not?)
who must speak only in a code
the Napoleonic? the Orwellian?
or as if the words were bouquets of flowers
arranged according to some inherent formalism
sounding a rhythmic castanet chatter

yet where do we find some urgency to communicate directly
something straight to the shoulder
to sum up and limn this pain
which doesn't go away
and which for some is so great they cry out
to penetrate this life which is done to us
in some conspiratorial faraway consultation
in which our interests are never taken into account
except as perhaps one of the "acceptable dead"
or a statistic of the percentage of those imprisoned
or one of those to be reported by Amnesty International
as disappeared

who can describe this grotesque farce of a life
and make it stick
force us to quake again as though reliving
its most awful and epiphanous moments
and wake up
how do we wake up
from the drowse of whatever niche
we have found to hide in
like some insect in a crack?

"no and i don't know where . . ."

"no and i don't know where . . ."
says this young gal about old enough
peeking around the door bare-shouldered
maybe the rest of her bare-assed
referring to my friends who it seems have flown the coop
interrupting her kid's or brother's mute stare
from under the window sash
up the stairs at one of those 407 and 1/2 addresses
or 603 and 7/8
upstairs over the storefronts
where the marginal people crib in these burgs
—leaving i notice a few children on the streets
about to be in the grips of their families
some desolate stillness gathering,
in the drab, gray dusk something pinched off
their separate nights falling as i remember
in this fading steel and farm town
"where they've gone . . ."

the boarded-up gas station on the way out
on the blind plywood eyes those classic reminders "fuck you"
    and "eat shit"
the way the proprietor of the candy store where i tried to phone
said "another day"
as he let down the awning at night
in that nasal sigh resigning,
when i asked if he had any soup
he pointed to the cans on the wall
and i didn't reply
but thinking my own fatalities

back on the road the next exit says Atalissa or Atlantis
the last of the horizon a serrated beach
some coast i am making for
shore still lit
but it embers out
keeps its distance, or gains it
as if it were going where we couldn't follow
to myself "that fucking town didn't even have a café"
the trucks turn on their running lights
signaling the loneliness of the old road night
the ones in front seeming to slow
the ones in back driving up your ass
"no and i don't know where . . ."

"so in evening there is still light"

so in evening there is still light
still gas to illumine these words
loneliness so commonplace like some dull pain
that one forgets to take account of
bad digestion or a crooked-up back
so fuck it, i say to myself
laugh a little—shrug—shake my head
laugh a little more
these conditions and how long through time
all the people strung out in this history
or those who were never in "history"
rather more than likely—
no special pleading it is said
so a thousand times over fuck it—as if we would try
to say with our hands
or could possibly express—
no one could invent a world like this
orchestrated by some half-heavenly, half-diabolical spirit
—but leaving us
it seems obliged to transmit
these lives lived out of the boundaries
that are only sustained in a desperate struggle
despite the official version of reality,
and we'll get them down too, by God
and be a long time croaking if we can help it
look around in the end with a worn-out laugh
fuck it give up the ghost

winter dawn

blue-dark, still
snow on roofs—levels of white
eddies blown up and off by delicate wind thrusts
—the light comes like a slow leak
now trees barely outlined mark solidity in plainer focus
shard of gold—early morning house-light, breakfast in the
    making
ticking awake of the frozen minutes
more light graying in—the dark blue mystery fading
readying for the daily round—or what you call it?
through back-alley walnuts
slant-roofed sheds upstanding,
tangle of weeds vibrating in the wind
knots where string lines tie
painter's dream of composition light and shadow
now day come
and this attempt—laid aside

"on some night a train . . ."

on some night a train is going past the library
and it seems gigantic tremendous with long metallic
    screechings
and this might be the night of loneliness's end
the library finally our world
with the books like souls breathing on the shelves yet silent
how we flow into this night like asteroids around a strange
    planet
and the people behind us, we have known them after all
loved them, more or less
enough so that it counted, so that we are no longer lonely
or   in the same way
and the bells on the train are beating intensely
but for me the books and the ones i will know
also ahead in time
as though we had a certain skeptical faith they might appear
and as Chestov says
even if we die like a dog under a hedge
we have made our mysterious mark in the world
and a few others have understood

in celebration of surviving

when senselessness has pounded you around on the ropes
and you're getting too old to hold out for the future
no work and running out of money,
and then you make a try after something that you know you
 won't get
and this long shot comes through on the stretch
in a photo finish of your heart's trepidation
then for a while
even when the chill factor of these prairie winters puts it at
 fifty below
you're warm and have that old feeling
of being a comer, though belated
in the crazy game of life

standing in the winter night
emptying the garbage and looking at the stars
you realize that although the odds are fantastically against you
when that single January shooting star
flung its wad in the maw of night
it was yours
and though the years are edged with crime and squalor
that second wind, or twenty-third
is coming strong
and for a time
perhaps a very short time
one lives as though in a golden envelope of light

for Juan Rulfo

it comes to you tonight
that you too are part of the world
unrecognized but still there
living somehow with the others
when you hear on the radio this night
a writer you had read years before
has died,
only two books
and has not published for thirty years
interviewing the translator
he said "well, he was the best,   that's all"
you hear the voices speaking from the grave again
so exact and full of the being of life
resonant, crotchety, and smooth all at once
"my problems," Rulfo said, "are time and space"
"and so by having the characters speak from the grave
I eliminated them, and this allowed
the characters to speak for themselves
without the interference of the author"

this laconic Mexicano a mystery to you
you pondered what he was driving at
with such spareness and ruin
and now perhaps you know a little better
"I did not even take space from the earth
for they buried me in your tomb,
I fit right well in the crook of your arm too
listen it's raining up there
it sounds as though someone were walking on us"

and so tonight this radio as it is called
which so often does not take account of lives
as strange and different as ours
broadcast from thousands of miles
some news that touched you in a way you cannot explain
and by tipping their hat to him
acknowledged you without knowing it
and while millions did not know of him
will shrug their shoulders and go to sleep
you think of him
working as a bureaucrat in the capital
struggling to find the spirit to write
sitting in the evening drinking his café con leche
in the plangent twilight and smoking a cigarette
as he gathered
in the curve of his brown and clifflike cheek
the silences, and let them brood—

men and women
(the Boltzmann distribution)

one after the other we consume one another
can't wait for the new conflagration
we eat each other alive
—afterward we no longer have any interest
in these soggy piles of ashes
for what promise could they hold?

behind us
like mile markers on a journey
little heaps of human rubble
like places where someone perished

we can never quite seem to fathom
the new ones we are always looking for
are someone else's burned-out buildings
—in some the mark of the arsonist
under the gay streamers

in our demeanors
we try not to betray
our ash memories
our personal Hiroshimas and Dresdens
yet sometimes a telltale look
swims up in our eyes

discard or be discarded
trash heap of the soul
smoking inner city of the psyche where the rivers burn

what's left—in these walking retreads
still smolders and sparks
becomes of gnawing interest
for at a certain point—when it's downhill toward death
—a tendency to poke around in each other's remains
as though half realizing
what's still alive? . . .
and the new ones don't seem so different
from the burned-over old ones
except for a certain way we fool ourselves
about this one being different perhaps
than all the rest

whether it could have happened differently
we can't say
but we would like to think so

the desperate

they come into your life
in retrospect
only for an extended moment,
long enough   to reach out
in their desperate quest

later you shake your head
thumbs out with your hands
shrug over and again
because you didn't know
they were going down
the third time
as they might have touched you

perhaps the desperate
recognize each other
and call out
in some muffled voice

but on what level
rests each of our despairs
and could they
be bridged?

then they are gone
fled in their descent
years later
word comes back

this one shot himself in the eye
that one was thrown
into the ocean
to get rid of his body

some, must be surviving
somewhere
but could we recognize them
if we could ever
find them again
or have they become
mute perhaps and unspeakably . . .
that glowing ember in their eye
is it still alive?

in the parking lot of the supermarket

riding in glittering machines they didn't build
walking blandly by in clothes they didn't fashion
with that vain air of imperialists at ease
going in to buy food they never grew, nor harvested, without
    realizing . . .
almost having forgotten that it comes from the dirt
that it once grew without its mulch of chemicals . . .
and these chemicals now lodging in their indifferent bodies

as if in their dim awareness they placed their trust
in the new computerized version of "reality"
"fascism with a data face"
to plasticize and homogenize everything to just the right
    consistency
as though they never crouched in the woods nervous and alert
wiped themselves with leaves

with the strange paper issue they pass back and forth
for various permissions
given and taken from them in wizardly fashion
stretched and shrunk beyond their ken
—and for those that can't get these paper pellets
by some slavery or submission
scam or respectability—a drone stripped of its functions
fit for furtive marauding in alleys
rummaging the garbage dumps

and us in our machine nearly rusted out
wearing our cast-off clothes indifferently
feeling peripherally the termite-busy to and froing at the edges
and our extreme marginality

as though we were the albino cockroach with luminous feelers
spies for some other way of life
which in this ant heap we can no longer quite remember
yet which rendered us individuals to some nth degree now
    dysfunctional
wondering what individual act to commit
what flares to send up
what crime of the personal to contemplate

instead we slink home to our lair
to rest and gather strength for the morning
for when the bees will darken the sill of the hive
and we must again pretend to be part of them
to hold to for a short time more
some vestigial surviving
until one day they find us
on the cross hairs of their focus
and we are recognized too plainly—
further exclusions against us will become necessary
for the health of the state

shocks brakes (for Kurt and Yansky)

as though seen among other competing nondescript signs
on some strip of waking bad dreams
like   steaks chops—
but which keeps winking out
and returning bloody neon
some ironic joke to ourselves
making us think of this life
of the aptness—no doubt
plenty of those—but how to withstand
to extract what can be salvaged
from the wreckage of human experience
from the various engagements
and near pummelings
and the few minor victories perhaps Pyrrhic

and i don't want my rear end to bounce forever either
as my mechanic friend comments on my car
hand pushing down on the trunk
as he says "it's one piece of shit after another"
but goes on fixing cars
and we go on down this ugly strip of life
thinking perhaps one day we'll begin to see, actually see
the weight of things
how they balance out the good from the bad
the dishonest from the real
or that it's all a dream everything is dreaming
that we must let the figments drift past
without such terror and desire

but how to find a focus on seeing
to steady our view
to find the courage which keeps getting lost
so that one day
in the face of shocks brakes
we can smile being equal to it

Nicaraguan journal

for Manuel Gonzalo, who spoke to us

the guy sat there barefoot on an old wooden bench
a *campesino* with a worn shirt
a soiled, broken baseball hat
his high-pitched eyes looking at us from out of the shadows
from a submerged stratum—some more primitive nexus
he had passed on the road the other day
when we were in the fields,
and smiled, seeming more quizzical than the others
curious and sympathetic
he had come from Jinotega in the west sixteen years before
had been mobilized during the revolution for six months up in
    the *montaña*
although he had no training he had fought without it—in the
    FSLN
which had been part of the United Front

from the curving muddy mountain roads the squat olive
    Russian trucks
came rumbling and bellowing up out of the darkness,
some of which turned out later to be Mack American
the shouting and the whistling, the slap and thump
of the *quintal* coffee bags, the shish of their being dumped
in the trough, the splat-dripping from the eaves
the loading platform lit only by a few bare electric bulbs
the almost fiesta or angrylike catcalling
diffuse waves of rain rolling in from the mountains above us
the roaring of the waterspout into the coffee wash under us
like some endless rushing into the delirium of history—
he called them *rojitos* ("ro-hee-toes")
"the little red ones" (referring to the coffee beans)

with a slow smile and a look of tenderness . . .
his feet looked as though they had been bare for years
and now their bunioned shape would not fit into shoes . . .
he spoke of the working class
and what it had meant for them . . .

the government-run textile factory we had visited . . .
they ran three shifts a day . . . had air-raid shelters
looking like subway entrances in the middle of fields
for when the Yankees came with their napalm bombs . . .
had their own day-care center
which stayed open for all three shifts
the children sang songs for us
something about hoping the war would end . . .
but we didn't really catch the Spanish
they had to tell us what it was about
but somehow you couldn't take your eyes off them
their innocence . . . then they sang in español
Old MacDonald had a farm eeii-eeii-oo . . .

the workers got one free meal a day in the middle of their shift
and all the overtime they wanted . . . still they told us
that a week's pay for the forty-hour shift
was enough to buy one of the better shirts they made
so the factory made cheaper shirts that they sold the workers
for about one-third that amount . . .
or they let them pay on time
the union rep who spoke to us was a woman, a Miskito
*   Indian . . .*

then he recited one of his poems for us
"how beautiful the morning
which brings us the day

how beautiful the coffee blossoms
yet more beautiful when they are picked . . ."
he spoke shyly and with hesitations
stopping then while the translator labored
and looking at us with some profound feeling
always using the formal *ustedes*
one of those who for most of his life
had learned it was better to have no opinion . . .
the rain was starting to drift in
over the partially open front wall

i thought of the kid outside of Matagalpa
who had hollered "fuck you" at us
as our bus went by
maybe it was all he knew of English
one or the other of us had said
but it was enough . . .

he said that before they didn't make much at all
and now they made more
but the prices had gone up
so in a sense it was the same
but now as it is said
"the peasants have reasons . . ."
that is, they know what they are fighting for
so that it makes all the difference

i had gone down to the stream to wash some clothes
she was already there with a couple of kids playing on the rocks
she had washed and squeezed out a pile already
and now she was washing herself
bare on top except for some primitive brassiere
which was not in the least opaque

she was soaping herself quite calmly in the sun
said "Hola" with a smile
i couldn't help but look over at her every so often
so without shame
without false modesty
so much of herself living and beautiful in the sun
"Buenos dias" she had said calmly and with kindness
as she gathered her clothes and children finally
and went back to her house

the trucks kept coming, beeping their horns with tremendous
    blasts
enough to jar the living wheat right out of you
no he didn't have a family
he was alone with God and his aged mother
only a year older than i, forty-nine
he looked much older, worn
some of the others seemed a bit standoffish
or so in their own worlds they couldn't reach to ours
or maybe they had seen many others like us
come and go in a few weeks
leaving them their long hours, monotonous diets
and possible death or wounding from Contra attacks
but this guy with his mashed cap
and who was an illiterate poet
had some feeling for solidarity
and even if we didn't amount to much as pickers
our quota was three *latas* a day
and hardly any of us made it;
most respectable *campesinos* could do six
and some *vanguardia* pickers made fifteen
even children could do two or three
the members of the UPE ("oopay"), the collective farm

couldn't understand why the *internationalistas*
and even the people from Managua
who came up as volunteers for the harvest
were such poor pickers
nonetheless he seemed to intuit
that we also had our reasons . . .

one of our responsables
had pointed out that the skinny dogs they had
were full of diseases and fleas
and were cursed and kept out of the houses
when they fought sometimes the peasants would look on with
     amusement
when one of the bitches went into heat and they fucked
the children would sometimes throw rocks at them
when they were stuck together
and make them dance a grotesque, yelping dance

he said speaking now with a kind of eloquence
that he knew the u.s. was a rich country
but it also had its poor
who must be as they had been
acorralado, corraled or driven
and they too must find an "opening"
as the Nicaraguans had done,
i had a vivid image of us as wild horses
breaking through a weak place in the fence
his voice would fray off to inaudibility over the water trace
but the translator would bring it back to us

in the museum of the revolution
you read how the Nicaraguans had struggled
to throw off the dictators and oppressive regimes

176

that we had supported since the 1890s
how we had intervened seven times in this century
to prop up one scumbag dictator or the other
Roosevelt had said "Somoza is a son of a bitch,
but he's our son of a bitch"
they quoted him in Spanish
"Somoza es un hijo de puta,
pero el es nuestro hijo de puta"[1]
how Sandino had been tricked and murdered
after being the only leader who had refused to give up
to the Marines
how wave after wave of different revolutionary groups
had been crushed and rubbed out
they had preserved some of the instruments of torture
Somoza had used in his dungeons
the FSLN had been founded mostly by the few survivors
of some other groups
who hadn't been murdered
and now of the original members whose pictures we saw
only three had survived the revolution
outside the museum they featured a baby tank
that Mussolini had given the elder Somoza as a present
it looked as though two adult tanks had mated
producing this offspring
but it hadn't grown up . . .
just the kind of thing Mussolini
would give a good friend of his for his birthday

the black autoworker from our group had said to him
that "our society must learn
from their peasant cooperatives

[1] " Samosa is a son of a whore, but he's our son of a whore"

how to civilize itself . . ."
Manuel nodded thoughtfully as though to say yes, perhaps
i thought of the irony, because that meant
that you had to consider for what a country was struggling
and not just their technical achievements
or the complexity of their social patterns

in the little mess hall, which was hardly more
than a closed-in porch
on the front of the cook shack
we had just gotten our sugared coffee, beans, and tortillas
she was standing by the end of our table
in the reserved silence they often seemed to keep
we noticed she had a big tin of, as it said, "Leche de polvo"
powdered milk, and we asked her
"para quién?" *for who, and she answered* "para los ninos"
for the children, and it clicked in you
that here was a concrete thing you could see the revolution
doing for them,
under the last Somoza, the women couldn't work in the coffee fields
now the women could work too
and they used the escuela *for a day-care*
so the children got their milk there
otherwise we hadn't seen a hairsbreadth of milk anywhere on the
    farm
since they now ate collectively on workdays
the women didn't have to take time out to cook meals
just then a new brigade—Brazilian or Costa Rican?
came in on the back of a truck up the hill
then we heard the chant for the first time
as they fiercely sang out
"Aqui, alla, Yankee morida,
Aqui, alla, Yankee morida . . ."

here, there or wherever, the Yankee will meet death
it struck strange chords in us
the history of our murderous meddling
the attack the ultimately expected . . .
and for which they were gearing up . . . (seven invasions already this
      century)
and that in some sense we were Yankees . . .
she looked at us then, realizing the strange discontinuity
of our identity, and laughed, then the cook laughed
the cook's assistant laughed, and we all laughed
holding briefly in that moment
beyond the barriers of our languages and cultures
an understanding of each other's strange but true positions,
national and personal,
and how ultimately absurd it all was . . .

with a kind of light in his eyes
he spoke, from out of the shadows of this history
"when you consider how long we have been fighting
for how many years
for decade after decade
how beautiful to think
that our country might find peace
that we might be able to work in tranquility
and not have to spill blood . . ."

he had been home visiting his people
somewhere out in the sticks
when the Contras came
while they held him and his father down
they raped his mother to death in front of them
then they slit his father's throat—
after that they hit him five times in the face with a machete
and shot him—left him for dead

but somehow he didn't die—
he was on leave from the Army
he had come up with a pal to volunteer for the coffee harvest

now he seemed happy as he told us
"when you came here to work with us
you came to join the working class,
the peasants, and the *campesinos*
and so although you may not understand it yet,
this is a great advance for the revolution
for now we are all together in some common struggle . . ."

but i wondered to what extent we were together
even in our small group of Americans
sometimes it seemed difficult to get along
or to see eye to eye, there seemed too much American in us
whatever that was
and we repelled each other like similarly charged particles
the differences in our backgrounds and outlooks
the tendency of our leaders to drift into authoritarianism
and of the group to go along with whatever they were told
the crowded living quarters, almost never being alone
the sicknesses that plagued us, the stress of the work
sometimes ragging us,
could we have made any kind of revolution I wondered
thought of the play by Peter Weiss, Marat/Sade
de Sade says "that's how they see your Revolution, Marat,
their soup's burnt and they shout for better soup
a woman finds her husband too short . . . she wants a taller one
a man's shoes pinch . . . but his neighbor's shoes fit comfortably
a poet runs out of poetry and desperately gropes for new images
for hours an angler casts his line . . . why aren't the fish biting
and so they join the revolution

thinking the revolution will give them everything:
a fish, a poem, new shoes, a new life
they storm the citadels and there they are
and everything is just the same—no fish biting, verses botched
shoes pinching, a worn and stinking partner in bed
and the soup burnt . . ."
even though you could like most of the people
it seemed hard to imagine if we were put to the test

but then i remembered with what kindness they treated me
when i was sick, and not making me feel guilty
that i couldn't go to the fields with them
how even though they came out of different circumstances
they seemed to grope about to try to understand each other
when we left they gave what they could of their common
    possessions
shirts, shoes, hats, clothes, whatever
for the Nicaraguans were in need of just about everything
you ended up admiring them in a sense
simply for being who they were, and trying in some way
perhaps they were the best of the lot
how is all this to be added up?
perhaps it was as Manuel said
we do not yet understand, how it is, or is to be
that we are really together in some common struggle

"before, we were constantly humiliated by the National Guard
they did what they wanted with us
we had no arms to defend ourselves . . ."
you could see the deep look of hurt in his face as he said this
"now we have a people's army to protect us,"

". . . the only hospital like it in the country unfortunately"
the guy said, "for people who had lost limbs,
since the war we're too crowded
only the ones from the provinces get to be inpatients"
. . . a series of connecting bungalows around a patio
you saw the technicians making artificial legs, prosthetic devices
the victims didn't look disturbed or vengeful as we came past,
they seemed calm . . .
perhaps only an edge of a question in their eyes
why does this strange gobierno
of yours want to blow off my leg?
but more a muted, pained puzzlement
most of the war-victims had stepped on Contra mines,
. . . suddenly entering one room . . . a strong-looking young guy
they had him up on his bed doing exercises to get a sense of balance
blown off above the knee—he looked resentful
that we were watching him now in his vulnerability
go away . . . his look seemed to say
now I have to learn to make do without my leg
it's hard enough without your watching
my fierce but awkward efforts . . .

he said now there are many news programs on the radio
and newspapers of various kinds
people follow the events of the day very closely
i wondered then if he could read
despite what the translator had told us
maybe he learned in the early literacy campaigns before the
    Contra war
because then he suggested that each of us write something,
    some message,
perhaps why we had come . . .
it seemed a strange request
yet it touched you in some way . . .

as though each of our messages or motivations
could rise above the general similarity of reasons and
    expressions
and be worth reading
he said that the people with a radio or a newspaper
shared these as they could with the others
or told them what they had read or heard

finally in the last days before going back
when politics and sickness had worn you down
you thought of the jungle evenings out at the collective farm
when just before dusk we played catch with the kids
someone had brought along an old football
and they would laugh as someone dropped it and it bounced crazily
or when one of us had to stretch out and be almost an acrobat
to catch it,
these were nearly the best times
with the children there was no more Somoza, no revolution
no Contras, no Norteamericanos, no Hegelian
dialectic of capitalism, the thesis, and Marxism,
the antithesis, it all became gibberish
fit for satire, no group dynamics . . .
only some being fundamentally human and easy
of laughing, and using your body . . .
a pleasant illusion which lasted only briefly

the last day we went to Granada
it was such a beautiful city they had canceled the revolution there
so as not to destroy their greatest treasure
(in Matagalpa you could still see the bulletholes
in the walls as you traveled through the city)
we swam in Lake Nicaragua off a little group of islands
and it almost seemed like some jungle garden of Eden

coming back, you watched the dusk fall over the landscape
now lush, then drier, more brushy, patches of strange, twisted trees
groves of jungle, dry arroyos, a few deciduous here and there
until you were almost alone with the forest and land
"No hay nadie, solomente los arboles"[2]

"in the end"
(and now he seemed to be almost entreating us)
"when you go back to your . . . beloved country"
and you felt the resonance as he spoke it
and only then understanding as it was echoed in the translation
that yes in some queer way it was your . . . beloved country
though you guessed not as beloved
as it might have been
"tell Mr. Reagan," and here he reminded me of my grandfather
who had also been an illiterate farmer
and who would speak with a strange respect and even awe
when he spoke of presidents or leaders,
"that despite all the suffering . . .
we will not give up
and we will not be beaten"

and you thought of the näiveté in the assumption
that we could actually approach our president
and speak to him human to human, or that he
would have any interest in our impressions,
or care about what we thought,
as perhaps he could now approach Ortega
at some meeting between the people and the Sandinistas
and say a few words . . .

[2]"there is nobody, only the trees" (Neruda)

he sat there smiling at us in the benign silence of his look
now again ensconced perfectly in his own world
the waterspout under us roaring into the coffee wash
giving us the feeling that for a moment
we might understand something, just a thread
the steadiness of the roar balancing it
but the delirium would go on
sweeping everything away
and us with it

FSLN: *Frente Sandinista de Liberacón Nacional*
quintal: 100 lbs.
ustedes: you
latas: buckets
responsables: leaders
escuela: school
gobierno: government

November dusk

mackerel riffs iron-filing toward the west
gray mattering of the brain's remembrance
splattered against the sky
Scomber Scombrous Japonicus
fish from the cold sea of our lives
providing our hand to mouth
all the luck i could have now
to have a can of it on the shelf

this somberness a refrain
and the red tatters of autumn
quickens the heart against death
while giving us an exact premonition
of its coming without hesitation

death coming with your eyes
in any car of the evening's unknown traffic

we wake to make love
in the long winter night already beginning
and drop off again, sleep saves us

then rise in the gray hardened morning
cast up on the barren shore
or our constant struggle to begin again

for Phil

we are talking about anxiety that comes up
from somewhere inside
you don't know where

warm as spring in late October
octubre
walking around, everything seems
open and free
easy and peaceful
lucky weather

talk about luck
in this life
a lot of bad
some good

count our money
4 cents he has
me a coupla dollars
eat in his classic old dump
of a rooming house
"something draws me to these places"
hamburger at grocery
a can of peas
one onion he fishes up
some bread i buy

here we are talking about things
a little disconcertedly
the warmth comes in the window
crumbling backs of buildings
giving us their dilapidated airs

other weird roomers
making their confined movements and noises
in that special "Dostoyevski behind a door" way,

opens and closes, you get caught
in the cell door
when the guard slams them all shut electronically
at ten sharp
crush your head

like life opening out springlike
into the yard
prison yard it was
where i walk the circle
with the other cons

spring evening in autumn
dwindle away
mysteriously filled
with sounds of trucks
where life goes to oblivion
caught just before Niagara
to rise and speak its common
almost unintelligible
song

"river of long standing . . ."

river of long standing, bridge abut-meant
surviving one long sunset of this world
walk the track one more time
outlived them all perhaps, lost
in the various rivers of this destruct
oh self-destructive
but which of us has really survived
who dead, or mad, or rust-caked?
strewn down the road
we no longer know each other
these mazy ways all hulked of iron
traffic of delusionary dream
all the sad mischances undergone
what weakness is this made
of tempered dream?
city of smoke casting its stacks windward
nothing come of all this machinery
except great railroad embankments
now the river whose ilk i know
in bones of thought
the trees haggard of man and flood
but still going on
even the stale end of prescribed day
gives way to my long last vision
day will come, and we take our chances
slim that they are
life also spins the wheel
catch up our throats in a last clasp
beginning to have its way
only here and there
along the vast esplanade of this sunset overhung
and downing green swift night

day born without a mouth

a despair that is silent
moves among the days
without speaking

merely a brother to the one who speaks
who has gone away on a voyage
but who will show up one day
in all the usual places

mornings the day's weather, human and otherwise
breaks over us
cold and remorseless

what can we say about events
that cannot even be described
the waste spewing into the river
the most articulate speech

along streets of evening
before darkened houses
on corners nondescript
and spotted with dirty snow
certain gestures are made
without echo
or response
i observe these hermetic formulations
and roll them into a sheaf of wheat
to make the bread
for those too strange to eat